Praise for *Value Prop*

"Jose Palomino not only points out the crucial significance of a value proposition, but also shows you how to create one—an extremely good one. His brutal honesty should be your cherished ally. His ideas are pure gold—no, even more valuable."

Jay Conrad Levinson
Author, Bestselling "Guerrilla Marketing" Book Series
With Over 20 million Sold

"*Value Prop* gets to the heart of what matters in competitive markets—why should customers do business with you? It is a guidebook that shows how to take complex products and services to market with a simple and powerful message that opens doors and leads to improved market share gain."

Michael Treacy, Treacy & Company Inc.,
Co-Author, *The Discipline of Market Leaders* and
Author, *Double-Digit Growth*

"Jose Palomino knows that the secret to effective communication is an understanding of how your products and services solve problems for customers. In *Value Prop*, he shows the importance of listening before you start selling. If you want to connect to your customers and stand out from the rest of the pack, follow Palomino's proven formula."

David Meerman Scott
Bestselling Author, *The New Rules of Marketing and PR*

"Palomino clearly articulates a straightforward way to build and communicate a promise to a specific target audience—an essential exercise that is too often undervalued or overlooked entirely."

Reed Cundiff, Senior Director,
Market Research, Microsoft Corporation

"An excellent, step by step approach for companies to honestly assess what they really have to offer and how to use it to win in the marketplace. *Value Prop* offers a practical and pragmatic transition of key messaging concepts into real-life selling situations."

Jack Ferraioli, Vice President,
Customer Relationship Development, Vertex Inc.

"A truly enjoyable read! It does a wonderful job of discussing value proposition development in the context of the entire marketing process. Great examples. Easy-to-read style. It makes a powerful connection between messaging and sales execution. As important, *Value Prop* provides readers with a roadmap for getting there. A key point it makes is the dramatic impact the development of effective "value props" and sales dialogue can have on close ratios, cost of sales and profitability. A sales force will improve results by applying the concepts in this book and drive real sales growth!"

Dan Ross, Executive Director,
Entrepreneurs Forum of Greater Philadelphia and
Long-time IT Industry Marketing and Sales Executive

"Palomino offers a refreshing strategy-to-action approach for executives seeking an immediate impact for their businesses. Company leaders can immediately begin using the I³ approach to revamp and improve their messaging, channel and sales programs in new and exciting ways."

Ed Wallace
Co-Author, *Creating Relational Capital* and
President of The Relational Capital Group

"*Value Prop* gives new and seasoned sales and marketing professionals the tools, incentive and encouragement they need to move their marketing message from the lost realm of the undifferentiated to becoming truly distinct and effective door openers and deal closers."

Richard Bailey
President, Client By Design, LLC and Contributing
Author, *Guerrilla Marketing on the Front Lines*

"The business world is littered with the bodies of companies that thought they had the next great product, but ignored the strategic necessity of a tight value proposition. This book is fantastic at taking the reader through a logical and powerful framework to maximize the value of your product and product messaging in crowded and confusing markets."

Bradley Hecht, COO,
Products and Services, Iconoculture, Inc., Former
Executive at Yankee Group, MIT and Gartner, Inc.

"The world is not run by those who are right; it is run by those who can convince others they are right. To win, you not only need to know HOW—you need to know WHY. In a very well written book, Palomino helps us understand WHY people choose what they choose and beautifully deals with the HOW of developing effective value propositions."

Jamshid Gharajedaghi
Managing Partner & CEO of Interact and
Original Contributor to Third Generation
Systems Thinking Methodology

"Clear, effective and easy to read, Jose Palomino has given the business world a gift in his first book, *Value Prop*. Real and dynamic differentiation for today's environment, grounded in efficacy and results, marketers and executives will want this on their bookshelves."

David G. Henkin
Author, *Conversation Innovation* and C-level Executive

"In *Value Prop*, Jose Palomino shows that he is an innovative marketer who's listening and practicing what he preaches. Read this book. Give a copy to a friend—especially if they have to survive and win in highly competitive markets. They will thank you for it!"

James Barnes, Chief Relationship Officer,
Vanguard Charitable Endowment Program

"In a world crowded with management books, Jose Palomino has done a remarkable job identifying, uncovering and simplifying indispensible truths about successfully bringing new products to market. This is the one book you need to read before you go to market."

Andre Taylor, Winning and Leadership Expert and Author of *You Can Still Win!*

"*Value Prop* cuts right to the chase: what's so great about your product or service and why should people buy it? Jose Palomino succinctly and effectively argues that without a compelling value proposition, there can be no differentiation and without a differentiated value proposition, sales and marketing will be uphill. If you read this book, you will get the shorthand version of what it takes to stand out in the market: *Value Prop* is a highly focused, practical guide to what is too often treated as mysterious and convoluted. This book is all you need."

Stephen J. Andriole, Ph.D., Professor of Business, Villanova University and Former SVP and CTO of Safeguard Scientifics, Inc. and CIGNA Corporation.

Value Prop

A set of promises, based on the capabilities and credibility of the offering party, that helps prospective customers understand how an offering uniquely addresses specific problems, opportunities and challenges.

www.ValueProp.com

Value Prop

CREATE POWERFUL
I³ VALUE PROPOSITIONS
TO ENTER AND WIN
NEW MARKETS

JOSE PALOMINO

Founder and President of g2m Group, Inc.

CODY ROCK PRESS  PHILADELPHIA

Cody Rock Press
info@codyrockpress.com

Printed in the United States of America
First Edition

ISBN 978-0-9819126-0-8

Book Design by Kimberly Coleman

To Carolina,

Thank you for our years together
and for introducing me to the
most important Love of all.

Jose

Acknowledgements

The many people deserving of my thanks would exceed the pages of this book. I would be remiss, however, if I did not acknowledge several specific individuals who made this work possible:

The memory of Tony Sacchitelli, my first true mentor, who said to me, "You're an entrepreneur—what the heck are you doing here?" And I have followed my entrepreneurial heart ever since.

My many true and fine friends who have supported my business endeavors with wise counsel and valuable time throughout the years.

My fellow Villanova MBA alumni, for so graciously supporting and encouraging me to finish this book.

My parents, Jose and Esther, who early on instilled in me a sense of "anything is possible" in America.

Special thanks to Elizabeth Hetzer, without whose careful assistance in capturing ideas and organizing concepts, this book would not exist and to Paul Wesman, who helped me get it over the goal line.

Thanks also to my children, Daniel, Amanda and David. Their patience and love have fueled me.

And most of all, to my partner in life, Carolina, who has always given me the freedom and encouragement to pursue and accomplish so many of my dreams—starting when she said, "Yes."

Preface

I love business, enjoy people, relish ideas and welcome new challenges. Throughout my career, I have found the most rewarding challenge to be generating new ideas, empowering people to act on those ideas and making business happen!

I have "made business happen" in marketing, sales and consulting roles with large and small companies, both market leaders and startups. That experience helps me look ahead to see a bright and promising future: **nearly unlimited opportunities for whoever can connect people's passions and powers to the creation of new products and services.**

Victor Hugo, famed author of *Les Misérables* and a keen observer of life wrote, "An invasion of armies can be resisted, but not an idea whose time has come." Where would we be without light bulbs, aspirin or the communication and transportation technologies we all too often take for granted?

Consider the simple pen. Whether writing inspiring words, drawing nature's beauty or designing buildings and airplanes, the pen has brought comfort to many and given expression to countless ideas—and someone had to make it and sell it!

I have been fortunate to work with many fine marketing and sales professionals over the last twenty-five years. I admire them greatly because they help bring great ideas to life, to market and into the hands of people who benefit from them.

That is what this book will help you do.

Jose Palomino
Newtown Square, PA
August 2008

How You Might Want to Use this Book

This book's ideas are primarily for companies going to market with a product or service and target market already in mind—whether a new product or service introduction or an attempt to enter a new market segment.

However, if you're at the stage where you have assets and capabilities (an idea, people and vertical market experience) and only a rough idea of what you might offer to whom—of course, this book will help you as well—but you'll need to invest more time and energy into understanding your target market and competitors.

In either case, this book gives you a **framework to diagnose your value proposition**: to make sure it reflects and delivers a powerful message to your **best audience**.

Read the first section, *The Value of a Value Proposition*, and you will know what to look for in a value proposition and why.

Read section two, *Creating Your Value Proposition*, to walk through a way of attacking the development (or re-development) of your value proposition.

Read the third and final sections, *Building the Bridge* and *The I³ Challenge*, and you will know how value propositions **connect and energize** sales conversations for big-ticket sales of products and services.

Or...

Take a break at your local Starbucks and read the whole thing.

I welcome and appreciate your comments or suggestions at jpalomino@valueprop.com.

Table of Contents

Your Message Matters

P roduct? Check! Pricing? Check! Placement? Check! Positioning? Check! **Value Prop?**

You have something you're offering—a product, service or combination—and you've identified your ideal market or markets. But do you know why they should care—why and how they would see the value in your offering?

Whether you're selling a new type of smart phone, a revolutionary airplane or a powerful new software application, the "tightness" or completeness of your value proposition is the single most important component of go-to-market readiness for you to shape and control.

Yet, how many companies fail to do just that?

By value proposition, I don't mean just the concept of what you're offering and to whom, but the carefully chosen words describing that offer as well. These words support your lead generation, advertising and marketing materials and they are the words your sales teams have to understand in order to connect powerfully with their clients and prospects.

Why does this matter so much? It matters because there are just too many words in circulation! As Dawn Hudson, Senior VP of Marketing for Pepsi put it, "The average American receives more than 3,000 marketing messages a day."

One way or another, **marketing messages** have unavoidably crept into almost every second of everyone's day and are part of almost all your activities. *Messaging* is overwhelming us from every angle in the worlds of business and consumers alike. To top it off, you need to create and deliver your own messages to your markets.

Yes, messaging is everywhere: **yours and your competitors.**

YOUR MESSAGE MATTERS

How will your company's voice stand out in this overwhelming chorus of messages? Introducing new products and services to new markets can be like jumping on a moving train: it's hard to do and can result in injury, dismemberment or death—to your bottom line.

Racing to keep up with the speed of business, industry change, globalization and unending waves of new technology, companies face an increasingly complex, competitive environment. On today's fast-paced business railway, a novel idea by itself is not enough to let you board the train. Speed and message execution (getting the structure and nuance of messaging right) are just as important, if not far more so.

Success hinges not only on the inherent quality of the product or service (the so-called "better mousetrap"), but also the ability to move swiftly, integrate resources and execute go-to-market tasks effectively and efficiently with a coherent and compelling message platform.

Companies such as Microsoft, GE and IBM can and do allocate massive resources to achieve ever-growing financial and market-share objectives. For younger and smaller companies, the challenges are many times greater and the stakes are much higher as survival often depends on your current marketing and sales programs.

Often, newer companies find that resource constraints—an outright lack of budget or skilled resources in corporate marketing, sales, product management and operations and, most likely, a lack of integration among those areas—hinder their efforts to grow sales and add customers.

The latter challenge, the integration of effort, is where even market leaders stumble, as technology analyst firm Gartner, Inc. noted in their assessment of the state of the high-tech industry just a few years ago: "Despite all the effort IT providers [*information technology vendors*] dedicate to go-to-market strategies and initiatives, the results often fall short of expectations. **In fact, these initiatives often conflict with one another.**"

The bottom line for companies selling business products and services is this: create a message platform that effectively communicates your offerings and enables coordinated efforts to reach target markets and achieve revenue and market-share targets.

Reality Check

As you explore this book's approach to creating an effective message platform, you will see how that platform has to include two key components:

- a powerful value proposition (concept and words) and

- talk-tracks or "cases" your direct sales team can use consistently.

For these to be "game changers" you must base them on your firm's realistic and reasonable potential: your real reality. Be sure your firm's strengths and background provide a strong foundation for the market-facing promises you make.

Know what you do well. Know what you need to improve. Know what you can do better than anyone else can. You have to know your own business inside out before even looking at competitors. It is critical that you connect the promises of your product offering to the reality of your organization.

The simple truth is that your specific offering (the actual products, services, promises and justifications you want prospects to understand) connects to and is affected by your company's overall identity. Your product offer has to be consistent with the strengths that your overall brand communicates to the marketplace. I'm not saying that you need to be *handcuffed* by your company's present reality, but certainly look at your company's credible short, mid and long-term potential—in the eyes of your target market.

Connect with your customers in new and more interactive ways. Listening carefully to them is not optional. According to many observers, including Alex Wipperfurth, author of *Brand Hijack*, customers are now in the driver's seat (not your marketing department) and this will continue to be the new way of marketing.

Customer perspectives and experiences define your brand, so it is imperative that the messages you communicate and the promises you make are consistent with the experience your solution actually offers to your customers. Offering ease of use, when your product requires weeks of training is an all-too-common inconsistency. It's as if marketing and product development never met.

Who Should Care?

Obviously, a message is nothing without an audience. In fact, the audience largely determines and defines the **meaning** of the message. In other words, *know your audience and how they're likely to receive and process your message.*

YOUR MESSAGE MATTERS

In business-to-business sales, knowing your audience involves understanding intricate stakeholder networks, both internal and external. Know who will be in the room at each stage of the game, receiving and questioning your message. Will it be the financial authority of your next big deal? Is it end-users interacting with your installation team?

Companies provide their salespeople with tools to navigate the complexities of the marketplace and prospect organizations. These tools include sales processes, CRM systems, extensive training and coaching. They also include overall marketing support to create brand and product awareness and lead generation. In fact, most complex-sales processes focus on pinpointing how individual sales reps should move from meeting to proposal to closing the deal. They identify categories of players as well as tactics to move deals forward through that process.

In addition to the question, "Who to contact?" implicit in that sales process, I suggest adding the question, "Who **should** care?" to help frame the relevancy of your messaging concepts.

This book doesn't offer an easy answer or simple shortcuts to market success. Rather, it offers a way of

VALUE PROP

identifying what makes your organization and its products and services valuable and communicating that value effectively to the right and necessary levels of your target buying organizations.

The Value of a
Value Proposition

*What to look for in a value
proposition and why.*

Start With the Truth

I f you build it, they will come.

With apologies to Kevin Costner, we have probably all learned by now that this is just not going to happen.

Certainly, you will probably start with "building it"—with creating an offering that has real substance. This fundamental truth, that you have something of value for your customer, is the basis of your business. If a product isn't great or distinct in some meaningful way, nothing else will help. But being great *is not enough*.

VALUE PROP

Being better is not enough. Even *being the best* is not enough.

*The imperative for today's companies is to build a stellar **message** to represent your stellar product in the marketplace.*

Again, this is not just "spin," as long as you start with something of real value. But, your product cannot and will not sell itself, no matter how good it is. Word-of-mouth (i.e., "buzz marketing") and other viral marketing techniques are not enough for business products and services. By definition these require much longer looks and buyer analysis.

Yet, your prospect is probably too busy to really study your offering carefully enough to see the relevant attributes that *you know* are so great. To reach your target audience effectively, you need to build a compelling story around your new product offering—a story that then becomes a powerful marketing *and* sales tool.

Building a story that effectively explains the truth or substance of your offering, and tells why your target market needs it, is the essence of creating a value proposition.

Using a concept I call "I³" to create a simple but comprehensive value proposition, you will effectively communicate your product's promises in terms of the three factors that I believe most influence buying decisions:

Innovation — what's new
Indispensability — what's useful
Inspiration — what's wow!

Complex sales are accomplished through one-on-one human communications, not brochures, websites, mission statements or any other marketing device, as important as these all are. So, your sales people need language and rationale to help them persuade other human beings that your value proposition addresses their primary needs and concerns. If you get the value proposition right, communicating the ways in which your offering is innovative, indispensable and inspiring, you'll have what you need to produce the tools for your direct sales force or strategic channel partners to get the job done.

A strong value proposition, then, is the basis from which you can develop a well-grounded marketing message that addresses the concerns of your specific customers within a target organization. Each of these individuals will be evaluating the purchasing decision against one or more hard criteria, including business, technical, competitive and financial factors, as well as against the demands of the decision-making process itself.

Applying your value proposition to the rigors of the buying process in this way is something I call building a Sales Case. (See diagram of the Message Platform, below.) The Sales Cases complete the message platform and toolkit your sales force needs to satisfy buyer concerns and turn a prospect into a customer.

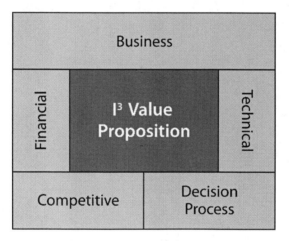

Message Platform

Don't make the mistake of going to market without a polished message platform—one that flows from brand, positioning, and tagline to business-focused cases, as well. Take the time to understand why the product is valuable to prospects and make a clear case as to why the product is innovative, indispensable and inspirational. We will see how in the next several chapters.

What is I³?

"You can't just ask customers what they want and then try to give that to them. By the time you get it built, they'll want something new."

—*Steve Jobs*

The I³ approach to developing value propositions gives you a foundation for your go-to-market initiatives. In the end, the I³ Value Proposition reaches out not just to a general audience, but sharply connects to your *optimal audience* with a precise results-driven message.

The I³ Value Proposition answers the questions— Why are we marketing this product in the first place? and Are we sure we're marketing it to the right audience?

This means taking a moment to *listen* before actually selling.

Defining "Value Proposition"

The definition of the phrase "value proposition" is sometimes a point of disagreement. Many marketers have defined it as a kind of "one size fits all" statement about a product or service. This fails to adequately recognize the consultative nature of complex sales practice.

That is why I have come to define value propositions as:

> A **set of promises**, based on the capabilities and credibility of the **offering party**, that helps **prospective customers** understand how an **offering** uniquely addresses **specific problems, opportunities** and **challenges**.

You can brand, position, price and place a product flawlessly, and still fall short in the marketplace if your overall value proposition does not powerfully connect with your intended customer. This is more than a branding

Capabilities
↓
Promises
↓
Target Market
↓
Market's Problems & Challenges

"tagline" or other high-concept exercise. It is the careful development of an offering and message to ensure the delivery of a value proposition that will influence its target audience—**because the promised value is true**—and the promised value is clearly presented.

The Elements of I³

The I³ Value Proposition describes the powerful connection your offering can have with your target customer. To develop your ability to deliver that message, you need to answer some questions:

- To what extent is your product *innovative*—**truly new**—*to your target audience?*

- To what extent is your product *indispensable*—**truly useful**—*to your target buyer?*

- To what extent is your product *inspirational*—**truly exciting**—*to your target market?*

Many companies create an **internally validated** value proposition (that is, with limited customer or external input) only to find later that *external* audiences had a very different view. In other words, their target customer saw nothing new, lastingly useful or exciting in the offering, in spite of the many fine features the company believed would prove compelling.

VALUE PROP

Respected high-tech industry thought leader Patricia B. Seybold, author of *Outside Innovation*, describes the shift away from looking at company offerings as products, but rather as solutions, something that gets a job done for the customer. Thus, it is about looking at the brand not only as a marketing tool but as part of an overall value experience. Product development, marketing and sales leadership must take an outside-in (vs. inside-out) look at innovation by focusing on what **solutions** customers *need*.

In a smaller company with a single product offering, brand identity and value proposition may be almost synonymous. One might argue that in this case, the promises implicit in the corporate brand are identical to the promises offered in the value proposition. On the other hand, brand is merely one element—albeit strategic—of the value proposition for a company with multiple product offerings.

Lessons from IBM

IBM is an unquestioned world-class brand and certainly one of the most famous in the world. IBM sells a wide range of products and services. Prospective customers assume that the products IBM brings to market implicitly possess the value of their well-earned reputation and respected brand.

THE VALUE OF A VALUE PROPOSITION

Yet, even IBM has sometimes fallen short when selling outside of its core strengths and has failed to understand the forces at work in their chosen markets. For example, the original IBM PC was a classic "skunk works" project led by the late IBM executive Philip Estridge, working out of borrowed IBM facilities in Boca Raton, Florida.

The resulting IBM PC was groundbreaking, not for its new technology, but for the way it established Microsoft's PC-DOS (later packaged as MS-DOS) and Intel's 8086 chip architecture as *de facto* standards. But, less than ten years later, in the early 1990s, the personal computing market was not embracing IBM's offerings, even after their great initial success. Why did the market shift? Was it just new competitors?

Despite possessing a world-renowned brand, IBM's personal computing products failed to maintain a connection with the broader market. The company followed up the original PC with the PC-AT, using the standard interfaces the market now expected. However, in 1987, IBM borrowed a page from their historic "big iron" playbook, and injected proprietary hardware (their Micro Channel Architecture) into the mix. All PS/2-branded PCs would now use this non-industry-standard, though technically superior, architecture.

VALUE PROP

At the time, IBM was the standard-bearer for large corporate computing. It sold many Micro Channel-equipped PCs to established corporate clients, but it had ensured its eventual non-relevancy in a market that was now being shaped by other competitors. Compaq, Dell, Gateway and others proceeded to grow market share, with the enthusiastic support of Intel and Microsoft.

IBM lacked an effective value proposition to connect its specific personal computing products to the broader personal computing market that was developing. What worked in one market reality—large corporate computing—would not be effective for the growing trend of distributed standards and microprocessor-based computing. Perhaps IBM realized it was not a "retail player" and the PC product category was not integral to its future.

However, the substantial advertising and marketing budgets it committed to the product family belie this point. IBM attempted to forestall this shift with their technically superior OS/2 operating system, which met a similar fate, resulting in a large write-off by IBM in the late 1990s. In the case of the IBM PC, the category matured, IBM's Micro-Channel was not broadly compatible, and Dell was successfully developing and delivering PCs via a superior, direct, business model.

THE VALUE OF A VALUE PROPOSITION

In commercial sales, the value proposition reaches far beyond brand and must promise a detailed, results-driven case as to why the customer should be so *inspired* by this *innovative* product offering that the product will prove to be *indispensable* to them. This is the essence of differentiation.

The Differentiation Dilemma

A value proposition is a promise of benefit. By itself, however, a value proposition does not necessarily possess promises that are unique or particularly exciting. Differentiation is what makes a value proposition effective or sellable. That's where the "I³ test" comes into play. Whatever you do, don't "spin" or convince yourself that your product is differentiated when it's not.

The simple reality is that there is little that is **truly new** or unrepeated in today's marketplace. That is, most innovation is an enhancement of current offerings (even the iPhone is an extension of cell-phone and MP3 player technology, the Dreamliner is another jetliner and most drugs are additional ways to solve similar problems, e.g., Viagra, Cialis and Levitra).

That is not to say that the age of innovation has ended—far from it. It simply means that the number and depth of fast-followers has reached such a level that new good ideas are copied seemingly overnight by many large and small competitors. You might ask, What can be done, if this is true? First, execution of an idea still matters: you can put two chefs in a kitchen with the same ingredients and yet only one whips up the award-winning meal.

Even in a highly competitive marketplace, differentiation is not impossible—it just takes a little more work. As mentioned, at any given time, there may not be many truly new or unduplicated offerings in the marketplace. This may sound obvious, but the most important point is this: make sure that yours really is different in some **important way**. This means a clear difference on some dimension that is meaningful to your target market.

Companies often don't even ask the question, Are we **really** different? and Are we different in a way that matters to our target market? Perhaps they are afraid of the truth or of the work involved in creating a genuinely distinctive offering. Instead, many companies and their marketing departments resort to "market-speak" to try to overcome product deficiencies —the "lipstick on a pig" syndrome. However, in the complex sale—where many savvy stakeholders are evaluating an investment/budget opportunity—"spin" will never compensate for what is missing: **a credible promise to solve a genuine problem in a new, useful and interesting way**.

So, What Differentiates?

For decades, leading companies could differentiate on quality. Quality, as defined by most buyers (product works without defect, as represented), is now a basic, or given, for most products in most markets. A good product is what customers expect today; you are probably not going to differentiate your product based on this dimension alone in most situations.

Lessons from Ford and Microsoft

Throughout the 1980s, Ford averaged two to three times more defects per 100 cars than Toyota or Honda. Today, Ford has crossed the quality threshold by reducing defects to well under 100 per 100 cars (defects identified within ninety days of purchase).

VALUE PROP

When it comes to quality, most consumers recognize Ford makes a credibly reliable car. Nonetheless, Ford continues to lose market share. Why? Because consumers are looking for design, options and performance across other dimensions in addition to quality—and Ford has not met the mark in those other areas.

Expectations are much higher than in the past and across more dimensions or feature categories in almost all markets. In 2006, Microsoft introduced its Zune music player with what can only be described as an underwhelming market entry[1]. The Zune is Microsoft's answer to Apple's iPod. The company brought the product to market with too little consumer advertising and PR and created almost no buzz whatsoever. The device had video, radio and many pundits agreed an even better price-to-value ratio than Apple's lineup.

Nevertheless, among other problems, the Zune did not prove innovative and indispensable in any major new and relevant way in a world already serviced by the iPod and other lower priced competitors[2].

Differentiating Commodities

Both Ford and Microsoft missed with these consumer-focused offerings—even with significant brand recognition and peerless marketing budgets. How can a business-focused product achieve differentiation?

Even more challenging, what if you are in a category that **appears** to have no opportunities for differentiation? In that case, you start with a solid grasp on the truth. Perhaps you are selling a commodity or near-commodity product or service. If your offering is late on the product life cycle of

introduction → growth → maturity → decline

then acknowledge that fact and work with what you have. Examine every point of possible differentiation and compare them to your competitors (see Prompter).

Differentiation Prompter			
	Our Offering	**Competitor 1**	**Competitor 2**
Speed			
Ease of Use			
Cost			
Cost over Time			
Training Required			
Compatibility			
Available Talent			
Support Policies			

Possible Dimensions

When you find an advantage, try to grow that advantage and drive that feature home. If you do not have meaningful or clear differentiators, then you **are** a commodity. This would mean competing primarily on price and should mean that your company has or is seeking primary cost advantages in its production.

Case in Point: Don

However, you can differentiate even a commodity product on something other than price and gain at least what we call "the right of last call." Let me illustrate with a simple example involving my long-time friend and early client, Don.

Don runs a regional chemical distribution company—a **commodity** chemical distribution company. He grew it from a "briefcase" operation to a large and important regional player, selling in a market that differentiates product by fractional pennies per pound. Yet, in spite of the fact that his was the smaller company, and that he offered no substantial intrinsic advantage in the product, Don developed a profitable and growing business.

How? He differentiated on customer service.

THE VALUE OF A VALUE PROPOSITION

This was before *Discipline of Market Leaders* helped popularize the notion of "Customer Intimacy." It was just Don's way to offer massive "TLC" to his customers.

Did this mean that these old-line purchasing managers simply accepted higher prices from Don? Of course not! But being the low-cost provider wasn't his competitive advantage. His advantage was being a pleasure to do business with and specializing in making their problems go away. While providing outstanding service in an old-line business may have allowed him to pick up a few extra fractional pennies per pound, what it really brought his firm was this: the **last call** a purchasing manager made before sourcing product. In effect, this was the right of last refusal on a sale at a given (commodity) price.

By providing high quality customer service in a business where this was generally unheard of, he gave people the reason they needed to give him their business. The power of this wasn't with any one sale, but over time. And, over time, Don built a successful business, receiving a small premium over competitors and with a reduced cost of sales.

Why were his costs reduced while offering better service? Don's approach positively affected his company's marketing and sales costs by having loyal and repeat customers—making that last call to his firm. Compare this with companies continuously scratching and clawing at prospects to net a single deal. The point here is simply this: even a "pennies per pound" business can find a way to be different.

Don was able to offer a new (for his industry) and surprising level of customer service: not hassling customers on replacing a damaged shipment or expediting an order at no additional cost, for example—all seemingly obvious things—but very inspiring for his market segment at the time. The bottom line is that simply *saying* your product is different is not the same as *being different* in a way that is meaningful to your target audience. We'll see later how a carefully developed I[3] Value Proposition can help you avoid being "all talk."

In a recent *Fortune* Magazine interview, Jim Stengel, chief marketing officer of Procter & Gamble, was asked, "It is very difficult to maintain a tangible product advantage for any length of time. Is that a problem for P&G?"

His answer is a classic rebuttal for any marketer despairing over their inability to differentiate their products and services: "No, it's not a problem. I hate it when someone says they're in a commodity category. We don't accept that there are any commodity categories. We are growing Charmin and Bounty very well, and if there is any category that people could say is a commodity, it's paper towels and tissues. We have developed tremendous equities, tremendous loyalties from our consumers. So, no, I think that is a cop-out. That is bad marketing and an excuse. We are not in any commodity categories."

Organizational Differentiation

Your current go-to-market emphasis probably centers on just a few of your offerings. Perhaps it's a new product launch or a relaunch of an underperforming line. No matter how much you may want to focus on the specific product being marketed and sold, the truth is that your offering carries with it the "DNA" of your organization.

The Discipline of Market Leaders offers one way to capture what that DNA looks like and the implications for your value proposition. Authors Michael Treacy and Fred Wiersema (and academics such as Michael Porter before them) describe three **value disciplines** by which a company can focus on how it wants customers to categorize or experience the company.

Since the publication of *Discipline*, much marketing thought has developed around the idea of leadership and differentiating companies around core competencies and corporate cultures.

The three value disciplines described by Treacy and Wiersema are:

- **Product Superiority**: These are companies that will continuously push the features of their offering to be faster, more powerful than competitors. This would be Intel and Apple for most of the last ten years.

- **Customer Intimacy:** These companies will focus on focus on understanding and communicating with customers very closely. They will look to delight their customers with service. In retail this is Nordstrom. In business services, this would be Bain or McKinsey consulting. In technology, there are fewer companies offering this today but IBM has the historic reputation for "getting it done" for its customers.

- **Operational Excellence / Low-Cost Provider:** These companies are continuously smashing cost out of their supply chain and offering customers the lowest overall cost in the category. Think Wal-Mart and McDonald's in everyday retail and Dell in personal computers[3].

THE VALUE OF A VALUE PROPOSITION

Treacy and Wiersema wrote that a company should choose to be an outstanding market leader in one of these three dimensions or "disciplines"; the other two dimensions would be supporting business factors and would have to be at least at whatever level is considered acceptable or baseline for a product category or industry.

For example, while McDonald's represents operational excellence (low-cost provider), customers still expect a warm and friendly greeting from the order taker. The baseline is such in fast food that "service with a growl" is below standard—even for a *dollar menu* purchase. Treacy and Wiersema make the case that winning organizations understand that they must double-down in one of these areas and cover their bets on the others[4]. This can result in standing above the crowd in a single dimension, without being found deficient (below acceptable) in the others.

Whether subscribing to the *Discipline* theory or some other guideline for your overall business model, understanding the focus of your organization will result in policies and an approach to marketing and delivery that give customers an experience that is consistent with the promise of your value proposition.

VALUE PROP

In other words, you'll be providing real things that deliver real value to real people. Of course, organizational differentiation affects programs and policies and the entire chain of connected activities that, together, make up your value delivery system.

The Value of a Value Proposition

A carefully crafted and integrated value proposition is simply the most effective and succinct way to describe the purpose and relevancy of your offering to a specific market.

When a company's leaders choose to launch a new product or service, they (should) have a specific market or markets in mind. Presumably, market intelligence and identifying unmet needs in the marketplace led to deciding to build and launch this new product. Your value proposition identifies the specific product and service benefits that most specifically meet those unmet (or underserved) needs.

You have to state the benefits of the new product to the target market in a way that will help them understand your offering as concisely as possible. You have to communicate the product's value to them with some urgency. Your company needs to assess what attributes will be of highest value to the target customer. This is the value proposition's "DNA" or **core message**.

In other words, a value proposition is the articulation of the **promises that your company is willing to fulfill for its target market**.

So why take the time to sharpen your value proposition? Why re-work an existing value concept and the words associated with it? After all, even the most sharply conceived and worded value proposition won't cast a "buy now!" spell over customers (although there are certainly times when one could hope for that ability). Your product is valuable only to the extent that your target customer **believes** it is.

This means that having a creative, grounded and well thought out value proposition, in concept and words, is not an end-point. Your value proposition is actually your primary marketing and sales tool aimed at

THE VALUE OF A VALUE PROPOSITION

a moving target: in motion with customers, their changing environment, needs and objectives. This can't be a static, or onetime effort.

This does not mean making assumptions about any specific customer's needs as there is no substitute for collaboratively solving a specific customer's problem. Great sales people meet customer challenges as an advocate and not an adversary—not simply looking to win something at the customer's expense or trying to shoe-horn a "wrong fit" for the sake of a single deal. A true solution-oriented sales process finds out what a particular prospect's issues are before assuming a situation-specific value proposition for that customer.

The successful sales mindset must be consultative: the value proposition should be matched to the needs of each customer. In order to find out these needs, a salesperson must have real and meaningful conversations with customers. (This is why it's critical to connect the I³ Value Proposition to the Sales Cases, as you will read later in this book.)

The value proposition has to state **what the product is and why it would be important to a particular market or customer.**

VALUE PROP

Your sales team has the challenge of finding out whether the value proposition is relevant to a particular customer, how to make it relevant and further, whether it will *continue* to be relevant in a market of similar customers.

To illustrate, the value proposition captures the promise of benefit for a specific market; your sales process has to apply these concepts and match them to the real needs of specific customers.

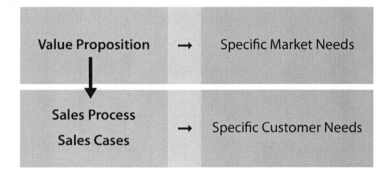

Creating Your
Value Proposition

*Walk through a way of attacking
the development (or re-development)
of **your** value proposition.*

First, Discover Your Value

Not everyone who picks up this, or any other business book, is going to be at the same exact point in the development of their business idea, plan or value proposition.

Earlier, I said that this book is primarily for people who already have a product or service and target market in mind. However, let's take a few pages to address what you might need to do if you are not quite at that point.

VALUE PROP

If you're sitting in a coffee shop with a yellow pad in front of you, sipping your latte as you stare out the window waiting for a million-dollar idea to appear in a vision, this book won't be of much help—at least not until you move from a blank page to a defined concept—however rough it might be.

Even better, if you at least have some real assets, such as a concrete idea, available talent, industry experience, and even the roughest plan for what you want to offer and to whom, you have something to work with.

You're at the point of being able to discover what value your proposed offering delivers and how it will fulfill its promise — the essentials of a value proposition.

You're ready to think about whether you have a real business concept that aligns with an unaddressed need in a real market and if you have the resources (or know what resources you still need to secure) to meet that need.

Often, business people become enamored of a feature they've added to an existing product or service category. An example of this would be General Motors and their OnStar initiative. The company added telematics[5] capabilities to each of their cars in the hopes that a now tech-savvy buying audience would choose their cars based on these capabilities. Executives even offered that the company's cars were now more an information appliance than transportation. Of course, the market was not moved by this position and GM has continued to suffer market share, revenue, profit and stock price losses.

Of equal importance, determine whether your concept—the value you plan on bringing to a specific market—will be entering relatively open competitive space or if you will be jostling competitors like commuters on the No. 1, Broadway Line subway in New York City.

The essence of discovering the value, then, is to look at all the interconnected parts of what you are selling. Namely, the products, services, support and anything else that a buyer will experience and associate with your offering. Michael Porter captures this "value chain" concept in his seminal book, *Competitive Advantage: Creating and Sustaining Superior Performance.*

To quote from the book, "Competitive advantage grows fundamentally out of value a firm is able to create for its buyers that exceeds the firm's cost of creating it." In other words, there are many steps along the way for a company to add value to a product before a buyer receives and uses it—and you have to be able to do so profitably.

VALUE PROP

For example, Dell has to integrate circuit boards, hard drive, screen and keyboard into a laptop before they can sell it. Further, Dell adds an intangible in the form of 800 number phone support, adding value to the package and distancing itself from competitors. Dell pioneered the use of the Internet to make procurement of multiple laptops easier and more hassle-free than it was with competitors. The value chain for Dell begins at the point of purchase through assembly and then to support. Dell also knew that to be a player in corporate computing, it would need to offer additional levels of service to add sufficient value so as to be compelling for the most demanding corporate buyers.

Discovering your value starts with an honest (sometimes brutal) assessment of what assets you have to work with. This does not mean that you are limited to what you can access today, but that gaps should be clear and filled in before you go to market. The prerequisite to discovering your value would likely be some concrete ideas, available talent, industry experience and some kind of plan for what you want to offer and to whom.

CREATING YOUR VALUE PROPOSITION

To make this a bit clearer, note the following Venn diagram.

Ideas and Resources:

- What "nugget" of an idea do I think I have?

- In what industries do you and your team (if you have one) have deep experience and credibility? Often, success comes to those who have a feel for the flow of things in a given industry—they can talk the talk and walk the walk with inherent credibility with other market players.

- What personnel do you have? Skills, experiences and culture can be critical parts of building out a value chain that delivers a distinct and winning offering to your market. Nordstrom hires for attitude and trains for product knowledge as their value to customers is in the shopping experience, and not the clothes purchased, *per se.*

- What unique intellectual property do we have? Patents, trademarks, processes: all of these are ways you can create and deliver value to your target market.

- How do you think your offering will change the status quo? Will your offering be revolutionary (Salesforce.com in sales automation) or evolutionary (a business software application for BlackBerry phones)?

Unaddressed Needs:

The above should provide clarity that can be applied against the next circle in the diagram. Specifically:

- Do you have clear ideas and a sense of what you bring to the game?

- Do you have insight into what needs are not being addressed by other vendors or even by your potential customers (for example, the social networking site, LinkedIn is being increasingly used for employment seeking and recruitment and is therefore addressing an unaddressed need: how to find a job or recruit an employee by leveraging personal contacts.)

CREATING YOUR VALUE PROPOSITION

Open Market Space:

- Do you have an appreciation of competitors?

- Do you know where the "open space" is in your target market?

- Do you know who and what your potential buyers are considering to solve the unaddressed problem? Many a start-up is launched to deal with a problem that is real and seemingly unaddressed, only to find a major competitor looming in the horizon. While it is nearly impossible to know a market completely and in all dimensions, it is essential for anyone developing a value chain (and committing resources and capital to do so) to know what else is out there for buyers to choose from.

Value Opportunity:

- The Value Opportunity is where you can add value to your potential customers, by leveraging your resources, their unaddressed needs and focusing on a space that competitors are not crowding (yet!). Just remember, no amount of craft or wordsmithing can overcome a value proposition that is fundamentally flawed: a fuzzy idea and inadequate or inappropriate resources aimed at either a previously addressed need or crowded market space.

VALUE PROP

Once you've discovered the value you could bring to market, the remaining chapters will help you take these ideas and sharpen your concept and craft a statement and foundational messages. With these in hand, you can go to market and communicate the essential importance, urgency and relevance of your value proposition.

I have developed a simple five-step process to create and support effective I^3 Value Propositions. Work through these steps once and you'll see how the process flows from rough idea to defined concept to a marketing resource you can't do without. It is a simple enough process to rework an existing value prop, or to continue refining a new one until it's market ready. (I recommend a final "simplification" step, as you will see shortly.)

1. First, you will **Frame the Value Proposition.** Develop the big picture of what each element of your I^3 Value Proposition offers to your specific target market.

2. Second, you will **Refine the Offering Concept**. Take your value proposition to the next level of detail by creating an **offering concept statement** that includes your specific product or service, the market you are targeting, the benefits they will receive from your product, and why your product is different.

3. Now, you'll be ready to **Test the Value Proposition** Challenge your I³ Value Proposition against the three core criteria, to see if your audience will really perceive your offering as innovative, indispensable and inspirational.

4. If the Test is favorable, it is important to **Support the Value Proposition**. Determine why *your company* should be viewed as the best choice to fulfill the promises in your value proposition.

5. **Adjust your Competitive Positioning**. Assess how potential customers will view your offering in light of competitors and alternatives. This is a "sanity check" step ensuring that you're aiming at the right market and have highlighted the aspects of your offering that are **most different** in **meaningful ways** to your customers.

Finally, at the end of each pass through your value prop there is something you must do...**simplify**. By simplify, I mean doing a few practical things that help get to the *pearl of great price* of your offering—the net-net "goodness" that will prove compelling to prospects.

You're going to need help and fresh perspectives. Engage as many key people as possible in developing and refining your value proposition. Establish an inter-active and holistic process that values the input and commitment of sales, operations, customer support, in addition to product management, marketing and exec-utive leadership. You must include key and trusted cus-tomers - and prepare to listen to their candid feedback. By this, I don't mean right before your product launch, but as early and often as possible, based on the quality and openness of your relationships.

These phases are iterative because you can't just go through the process once and think you're done. With so many factors continually shifting in the market-place—technology, competitive landscape, economic cli-mate, corporate strategies, etc.—a value proposition may only have about a twelve-month life-span, requir-ing a nearly continual cycle of monitoring and adjust-ment.

The next chapters will walk you through each of these five phases, showing you exactly how to develop your I^3 Value Proposition.

Frame Your Proposition

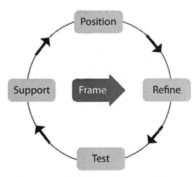

Creating I³ Value Propositions

To frame means to "rough sketch" your ideas. It means that you don't have to have a perfect idea or complete information to begin. Get started with a clear vision of your target market. Exactly whom are you targeting?

VALUE PROP

For example, are you going after companies with particular combinations of the following factors?

- Company type (size, employee count, etc.);

- Industry (financial services, high technology, healthcare, etc.);

- Culture (young & hip vs. old-line and establishment);

- Geography (local, regional, national, international or a region within a country);

- Targeted key contact position (CEO, CMO, Sales VP?).

More importantly, think about what you're offering as a hypothesis. In other words, think about your offering along the following lines:

What do we do (or offer) that has a distinct value (benefits) for a specific type of buyer (either a title in a type of company or a general target business, as bulleted above).

Sometimes, this means re-thinking what's worked so far—especially if it's stopped working. For instance, a long-time client backed into success more or less by accident. They are a well-respected web design firm that

CREATING YOUR VALUE PROPOSITION

recovered from the "dot bomb" in an unexpected way.

When we looked at their passion and favorite clients, we found many types of companies: tech focused, financial institutions and large not-for-profits. We asked them in which of these sectors did they see the fewest obvious competitors. They felt that the larger not-for-profits were the hardest to penetrate and many web design firms preferred the faster pace of other industries. These not-for-profit organizations were loyal, had budget and rewarded vendors who engaged with them in a patient (long) sales cycle. The company leveraged this epiphany into renewed growth by further cultivating these relationships and networking into new ones.

For them, framing their proposition meant stating something like this: "We deliver best-in-class web design services for larger, mostly education-focused not-for-profits."

The goal of framing your proposition is not to "nail it," but to stake out a starting point to create the language you will refine, test, support and position. More specifically, "framing" means developing a *30,000-foot view* of how your offering is Innovative, Indispensable and Inspirational ("I³") and doing so in terms that are understandable and exciting to your specific target market.

Let's walk through the three dimensions of an I^3 Value Proposition.

Innovative: A New Twist

To grab your target customer's attention, you have to offer your product as new, or at least as a significant new twist on an existing product or product category. Mere line or "flavor" extensions are not typically new enough, from an I^3 point of view.

Lessons From Apple's iPod

An example of an I^3 Value Proposition we've all seen and many have admired since its launch in 2001, Apple's iPod has arguably proven itself as the single greatest consumer product success of recent times. With over 100 million products integrated into the lifestyles of loyal users as of this writing, Apple has reinvigorated and redefined the music industry.

Though Apple's iPod was not the first MP3-type music device to market, it changed the face of MP3 usability and consumer acceptance of the technology and its possibilities.

Unlike its predecessors, Apple innovated the **overall experience** for music listening and the iPod successfully blended technology into an easy-to-use MP3 player format. Consumers were able to look at personal music storage and listening in a new way—easy, integrated, cost-effective and enjoyable—with minimum frustration.

The iPod's I³ Value Proposition

Innovative: New to Target Market	Indispensable: Highly Useful	Inspirational: WOW! Design
An Exciting New Way to Capture Your Musical Life. .99 cents per song – unbundled songs from albums Smaller; higher capacity Full and easy integration with Macs and PCs	Fully Replacing Your Present System of CDs and CD Players. "Rip" and forget Ability to buy that one song Never carry CDs again!	Hip—Cool—Beautiful Executed with Superior Ergonomics and Ease of Use. An Exciting Product to Use—A Feel of Absolute Quality in Your Hands. Wow—I can buy that one song! Sounds great!

"Innovation" cannot just be a buzzword used in product development, but rather must be a connection to the mind of the customer based on something truly new to their experience. Innovation is not gimmicky or trendy, although it may certainly have some added "flavoring." Whether that added flavor truly adds value largely determines the success of the innovation.

VALUE PROP

Former Intel Corp. Chairman, Andy Grove, comments, "In my view, the word innovation has become overused, clichéd and meaningless. I detest the mechanism that spits [such fads] up because they are so much easier to talk about than to do."

So, what is innovation in the context of a complex sale? After recently attending several major high-tech trade shows, I observed that if all exhibitors pooled their marketing collateral and mixed it up, no one would notice any differences. This kind of me-too-ism is anti-innovation.

To be innovative doesn't necessarily mean being revolutionary, which is perhaps too high a standard, or even new technology that is unique and *completely unduplicated*, although achieving this level of innovation is naturally a plus. Rather, it means that **how** your firm and its products solve a problem is new, fresh and uncommon to the specific markets you're addressing.

Innovation is the critical solution focus for creating distance from your competitors. Done well, Innovation elicits the observation: *I have never seen that before.*

Lessons in Innovation From Waters AcQuity
In 2004, the Waters Company introduced a product called the Waters AcQuity UPLC. It was a device that

improves chemical testing times (called chromatographic run times) for scientists in laboratories. The company's commitment to real innovation resulted in a solution that proved to be the most efficient in the industry.

Waters' divisional president Art Caputo said, "It all adds up to productivity, making scientists more efficient, allowing them to do more with the time they have. Our customers are in a race. And the rewards go to those who reach the finish line first with a new drug, or who can release a product from manufacturing faster."

The firm's innovation was a direct value to the customer, meeting a real business need. Consequently, this was the foundation of a solid value proposition, one that could claim that their product was both indispensable, getting more done in less time, and inspirational—helping the user to win the race.

Indispensable: Truly Useful

It is not enough for customers to recognize your product is innovative or new. It is **as important** to communicate how it is *truly useful*—to an extent that it becomes *indispensable* (useful over the long term), as well.

VALUE PROP

The "Indispensable" factor answers the following questions:

- Who needs this product?

- Why is it useful to them?

- To what degree will it affect the daily operations of my target customers?

- Most importantly, to what degree would *not* having this have a significant negative impact on my target customer?

Indispensability is not necessarily an implicit quality of innovative product offerings. Indispensable products live past the initial innovative stage: they are indispensable in the context of their intended use; they are not just passing fads. **Their utility is a persistent quality**.

Lessons in Indispensability From Salesforce.com

Salesforce.com was founded in 1999, offering online customer relationship management services on a hosted, monthly subscription basis. At a price of $50 per month for the first five users and $50 per month for each additional user, and easy access through a Web browser, the firm provided a no-risk way for smaller companies to gain the functionality of enterprise software applications at a much lower price point.

The offering was scalable, easy to use, and demonstrably *indispensable*, especially to customers who did not want to buy and maintain traditional computing resources. By taking advantage of trends in the software industry and using genuine innovation to address the needs of their target market, Salesforce.com has become the new face of Internet software and taken a leadership position in the market.

Indispensability is also utility at the highest possible level. In high-tech, this means discovering and developing this quality through a process of matching features to requirements. Unlike consumer impulse purchases, business products and services are often committee purchases, so these attributes have to survive intense multi-disciplinary review.

You can illustrate indispensability/utility by grabbing a prospect's interest with a solution that zeroes in on a core problem. Why is your product useful in solving that problem? To whom? In what context? What other problems does it solve? What are other benefits to the buyer that your offering provides? How long will it deliver these benefits?

Indispensability usually means **easily integrated**. To put it another way, a solution is useful to the degree it is actually used. A great new software product that is incompatible with existing systems is not useful, although it may in the abstract have wonderful attributes. Of course, organizations will purchase incompatible or hard-to-integrate technology for specific purposes, if the technology's features are not available any other way, but this is costly, time-consuming and a hard decision to make.

We could illustrate Indispensability with a simple formula:

**Indispensability =
(True Utility x Useful Time) x Ease of Integration**

The more **truly useful** a product or service is, and the longer the **time its utility is realized** and the **easier the integration** effort for a customer to receive the benefit of that utility, the **greater the indispensability** of the offering.

Lessons From Segway

To illustrate the flip side of the indispensability dimension, let's look at Segway's Human Transporter, introduced with much fanfare in late 2001 and with no less a mission than revolutionizing the world of transportation. Dean Kamen, the inventor of this "super-scooter," expected to see the product integrated into the U.S. Postal Service, FedEx and everyday consumers' lives. In short, the Segway was going to change the world. Most analysts, technology watchers and business writers acknowledged the amazing wizardry of this engineering marvel. Using gyroscopes, onboard computers and light-weight materials, Kamen created a truly innovative product. What happened?

First, it appeared that the $5,000 entry price was too high for an unknown and unproven product. Second, and more importantly, what problem was it solving? For the better part of a century, Americans have voted: cars win! Indispensability should mean that your target customer "gets it" and understands why your product is truly useful over the long haul—and why it is **more** useful than the status quo.

The innovation or "newness" of this product simply wasn't enough. Jim Norrod, Segway's President offered, *"Our lesson learned is that it's easier coming up with innovative tech than it is to change people's behavior."* As it turns out, the innovative and inspirational attributes of the Segway simply weren't enough to change the way people were doing things.

VALUE PROP

Ask yourself: *To what extent can you convey the message that your product is indispensable to the needs of your prospective customer? How will you weave it into your customer's daily grind? Will it offer lasting and substantive utility?*

Inspirational—WOW!

Now, given that your offering is new (innovative) and truly useful over time (indispensable), the remaining step to having a powerful value proposition is to ask the question: *is there anything exciting (inspirational) about our offering?*

Inspiration may be the most difficult I^3 factor to pinpoint and specifically prove: in short, the "WOW!" factor. The inspirational aspects of your value proposition speak primarily to design excellence by translating innovation and indispensability into something exciting. It is an integral part of developing a complete and compelling value proposition.

Inspiration and design excellence target the knowledgeable observer who looks at your product and says *"Wow, it's incredible that they managed to do that!"* This means designing the product so well that it elicits admiration from a fellow practitioner of the art (a Ford engineer admiring a new Porsche, for example).

CREATING YOUR VALUE PROPOSITION

When you step into an Apple company store, the beautifully coordinated industrial design of both the space and the company's products creates an inspirational experience for prospective customers. The attention to detail and obviously superior craftsmanship inspires a belief that the products offered must be better, different and more desirable than any available elsewhere. Procter & Gamble's VP of design innovation and strategy, Claudia Kotchka, says, "Design thinking can work in any business and in any function." And this certainly includes complex and big-ticket products and services.

You need to ask yourself some design-related questions: To what degree does the experience and design of your product offering motivate your customer to purchase? Is your product design consistent with your branding message? Does your product inspire a "Wow!" Is your product's design the *tipping point* for the decision-making process?

How important is this in practical terms? Jim Wicks, director of consumer-experience design for Motorola recently stated, "We want to create one iconic design a year." The business press has highlighted design excellence over the last several years—often noting how excellent design is now a "point of entry" attribute for common products. Business-to-business markets increasingly expect design excellence and organizations are less receptive to building, modifying and otherwise retrofitting solutions. A clear example of this trend is enterprise business software, with the growing acceptance and expectation of SOA (Service Oriented Architecture)[6] and SaaS (Software as a Service)[7] based applications—systems that work well and, ideally, seamlessly with one another.

Inspirational focuses more on the manner in which your product solves a problem—your product's distinct and exciting way of doing what it does. Perhaps the "inspiration factor" comes from the fact that your company has come up with a solution to a problem in the first place (think HTML browsers circa 1995).

Apple products are not only functionally innovative, but they are perhaps the best example of inspirational design for complex consumer products. Though Apple's designs are consumer focused, their success has stoked an appetite for excellent design for all technology products.

In Apple's case, their design excellence makes customers want to purchase their products—the smooth, compact, elegant nature of their products embody the message that the iPod is simple, easy to use and "cool."

However, design excellence is not just a consumer issue. Corporate buyers have had to contend with long training curves and personnel turnover expenses in the use of ERP, CRM and other business software applications. The process of hiring consultants, law firms, ad agencies or CPA firms—establishing criteria and selection interviews—often takes months to complete. These purchases all too often mean hassle, confusion and a lot of work on the part of clients.

Simply, business products and services are delivered in ways that either vex or thrill customers, often depending on the number and length of steps between a decision to buy and the ability to realize the benefits of that decision. Treat these as consumer-marketing-only attributes at your own risk.

After all, corporate buyers live in the real world and expect those things for which they authorize millions of dollars to work at least as well as those things they purchase for a few hundred dollars at the mall. Whether its a new laptop from HP or a new RAID storage server from Network Appliance, buyers want to be impressed.

Lessons in Inspiration From Boeing's 787 Dreamliner

Boeing's 787 Dreamliner is a model of inspirational design—it isn't just better—but was built with a specific design vision to impress buyers.

In their review of the 787's introduction, Time Magazine observed of the fanfare,

> ...*few at Boeing, if any, would argue that it wasn't worth it. As the hands of Boeing's workers graced the final product on Sunday, checking out the landing gear, the fasteners, the smooth sides that lacked the ripples often caused by aluminum, many stood back to admire the craftsmanship of so many countries combined.*

> *"Boeing's brand reputation in the last six months has been transformed because of this plane," says Paul Charles, director of communications for Virgin Atlantic, which has ordered 23 787-9s for delivery from 2011. "It's in the same league as the Wright Brothers' wooden plane, the first metal plane. And this is the first plastic plane," he says. "This is precisely the kind of milestone in the industry that we need."*

Inspirational, indeed[8].

Lessons From Craigslist.com

While inspiration is rooted in design excellence, it also includes solution elements—perhaps surprising notions in the realms of price, speed, cost-effectiveness, affordability or security. Not every product will have all of these radical elements, but perhaps one is enough to elicit a "wow" from your target market.

Craigslist, for instance, has built its value proposition largely on the inspirational quality of integrity, with no catches and with a genuine, honest focus on the interests of its community of users. The company serves 450 cities with 750,000 job listings and 14 million new classifieds per month. Craigslist generates revenue by charging nominal fees for job posts in seven cities and for brokers' apartment listings in New York. There are no banner ads or user fees. The site became profitable in 1999, and analysts estimate the site took in $25 million in revenues in 2006.

Craigslist was profitable, but its focus was not all about the money—at least not from charging visitors to their site. The firm knew that trying to make more profit by simply selling more advertising would drive some users away. They knew they serve a community of regular users and have perfected the art of listening to them. People find this refreshing and inspirational[9].

At some point, you have to answer the question: *Why would anyone look at our offering and say "WOW!?"*

The stronger an element is as an I^3 dimension, the more the product is a "no-brainer" purchase for customers and will sell faster and save your company time and money while delivering increased top-line results.

Framing the I³ Value Proposition

The chart below is an I³ "prompter" designed to get you thinking about your offering in I³ terms.

I³	Innovative	Indispensible	Inspirational
1. Core Offering	What we offer that is **new**—in the following way…	What we offer is **useful** because…	What we are providing is **exciting** because…
2. Core Offering for Specific Market	What we offer is **new** to this market.	What we offer is **particularly useful** to this market.	What we are providing is **exciting** to this market because…
3. Offering to Specific Market in Combination with Something Else	What we offer is **new** to this market when **combined** with (partner, other product, added service offering)	What we offer is **particularly useful** for this market when **combined** with….	What we are providing, in **combination** with "XYZ" is **exciting** to this market because…

1. Think about what your offer is in its most **direct and simply descriptive terms**. What is it and why is it Innovative, Indispensable and Inspirational?

CREATING YOUR VALUE PROPOSITION

2. Now, place this core offering concept in a **specific market context**—either your historical market or one you're targeting—ask the same questions and notice any differences that are market specific. These will pop up as relative strengths or weaknesses for your product in that specific market.

3. Lastly, think in terms of a key **value-added or channel partner** and see what shows up. This means your core offering + target market + partner (value add or channel).

Remember, at this point you're "framing" your value proposition. That is, you have started articulating how your product or service (or combination) delivers value to a specific market in a new, useful and exciting way. This is your starting point—and you should have a sense that it "rings true"—at least as a basic idea.

Refine Your Offering Concept

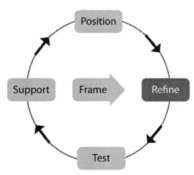

Creating I³ Value Propositions

A fter initially framing your value proposition for a specific target market, create a succinct but thorough **offering concept statement**.

This statement outlines:

- The specific product or service you offer;

- The market to whom you're offering your product;

- The benefit derived from using your product;

- Why and how your product is different.

Here's an example: *"We offer pre-acquisition IT consulting services to venture capitalists, reducing the risk of unseen technology-related liabilities in target companies and enhancing the accuracy of deal valuation, by conducting comprehensive, business-savvy IT due diligence."*

While this sounds like a mouthful—it captures the essential moving parts of what this firm offers, to whom and why they should care. It will get whittled down and refined as you move forward, but for now it serves as a placeholder for the key ideas of your value proposition.

The Art and Science of Targeting a Market

According to Merriam-Webster's Collegiate Dictionary (Tenth Edition), a hypothesis is:

"an assumption or concession made for the sake of argument; an interpretation of a practical situation or condition taken as the ground for action."

CREATING YOUR VALUE PROPOSITION

The identification of a target market begins with a simple hypothesis, captured in your offering concept statement. Keep the statement as concise and brief as possible. Focus on breaking down the offering and its value to the simplest, most direct terms. Think of the offering concept statement as a train of connected and inseparable ideas:

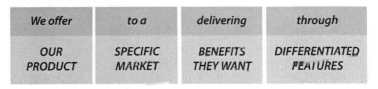

We offer	to a	delivering	through
OUR PRODUCT	SPECIFIC MARKET	BENEFITS THEY WANT	DIFFERENTIATED FEATURES

Translated into a simple statement, it becomes:

We offer OUR PRODUCT to SPECIFIC MARKET delivering BENEFITS THEY WANT through DIFFERENTIATED FEATURES.

At its core, the selection of a target market is part of a **continual** hypothesis, beginning first with an assumption that your product and its value proposition will be relevant to a particular group of customers. The job of your marketing and sales specialists is to argue for and against this hypothesis and determine its validity through research, testing and real-life experience.

Testing the Offering Concept Statement

Test the Offering Concept Statement carefully to ensure that its logic holds up. You can do this with something I call the Offering Corollary[10]. The Offering Corollary rearranges the elements of the hypothesis to see if they still make sense and sound as compelling as before.

Version "A" tests whether the removal of your offer from your target market is the same as removing the benefits that market seeks.

Version "B" tests whether your DIFFERENTIATED FEATURES are truly required to deliver the DESIRED BENEFITS.

Version "C" tests whether your TARGET MARKET even requires your offering's BENEFITS.

CREATING YOUR VALUE PROPOSITION

The following illustrates all three:

The Offering Concept Statement	The Offering Corollary
We offer OUR PRODUCT to OUR SPECIFIC (TARGET) MARKET delivering BENEFITS THEY WANT through DIFFERENTIATED FEATURES	**Version A:** Without OUR PRODUCT, the SPECIFIC MARKET would **not** realize DESIRED BENEFITS. **Version B:** The SPECIFIC MARKET would **not** realize DESIRED BENEFITS without our DIFFERENTIATED FEATURES. **Version C:** The SPECIFIC MARKET **requires** the DESIRED BENEFITS.

An example of applying Version A to the sample concept statement given earlier would be as follows:

"Without our IT consulting services, a venture capitalist risks finding unexpected technological liabilities in an acquired company and paying too high a purchase price."

Write out all three Corollary versions of your offering concept statement and determine whether those statements are credible. If The Offering Corollary does not pass the "sniff test"— if you don't get a good feeling about it—then you may have a miss: an Offering Concept Statement even you don't believe.

VALUE PROP

If the hypothesis appears to be logical and verifiable, it becomes grounds to continue refining your concept. Yet, you are still at a tentative and conditional point, because everything still rests on the answers to three questions:

- Will your target market's current situation in the marketplace be conducive to wanting your offering?

- Will your target customers find value in your product product offering?

- Will they value your product enough to pay what you require?

Like all hypotheses, yours must be continually tested, verified and modified, until you're confident enough to make strategic decisions and resource commitments to support it as a cornerstone of your go-to-market efforts.

Market Focus, But With Caution

Naturally, an established company will identify target markets based on its historic strengths. While market focus is a competitive strength, it can, however, also be a limiter, especially when looking at a new product launch. The adage, "to the hammer, every problem is a nail" is especially true in large commercial sales. To mainframe computer manufacturers in the 1970s and

CREATING YOUR VALUE PROPOSITION

1980s (IBM, Amdahl, Unisys and others), smaller businesses represented a "time-sharing" opportunity.

This view was exploited by mini-computer manufacturers (Digital Equipment, Wang, Prime and others) growing in mid-and-specialty markets during that time. Ironically, but somewhat predictably, this new group viewed PCs as underpowered and "strictly personal" computers. Consequently, they missed the networking opportunity inherent in the PC world, which eventually led to their demise or acquisition (e.g., Compaq acquired Digital Equipment and Tandem Computers and HP acquired Compaq a few years later).

It is possible and necessary at times to break out of your traditional target market and take a leap into a new pool of potential customers, but you must remember to stay grounded on the facts as they are now.

Matching Your Capabilities With Market Needs

Your **real capabilities** should drive your selection of a target market, not dreams, hopes or catchy slogans. When identifying a target market, you have to understand what it is that you are offering and how the attributes of your offering are relevant in that marketplace. Capture the attributes of your product today. Build a messaging platform on what you actually have (see Start with the Truth.)

Remember that you cannot and will not sell what you do not have. Spin may be in, but smart buyers know the difference.

This is not a recommendation to avoid innovation or "pushing the envelope," but to focus on *true messaging*: effectively communicating the **reality** of your differentiation. If market testing and analysis point to a needed new feature or function, then make a decision: sell today's offering now; wait to add the key feature or sell today's features now based on how they deliver value. Refine your product plans as soon as possible, as "market time" is best thought of as operating with a fast clock.

Once you have identified markets your capabilities best serve, look at the coverage of those markets and the competition in each particular market. Are you bold enough to go against existing competitors? Is your value proposition strong enough? Will you attempt to find a niche within a less-established market? Matching capabilities with market needs is the essence of refining your value proposition and making it truly distinct.

CREATING YOUR VALUE PROPOSITION

Testing Market Interest

The process of "testing" market interest within the complex sales arena is quite different from testing the market for consumer goods, so it's important that you back up your selection of target market with the highest quality research you can afford. For a smaller company this might mean aggressive "Googling" while a mature or larger company might commission custom research from industry analysts or other specialized consultants. Initially, you'll do more market testing as you roll forward in this—and it is essential that you sharpen your message with insights from your research.

Specifically, test and verify your hypothesis with research surrounding the relevance of your I³ Value Proposition. This means surveys, research advisory relationships (i.e., Gartner, Yankee, Forrester, etc.) and other industry experts who can further refine your value proposition. Simply put, a discussion with the right "player" around the question, "have you seen anything like this before?" could provide invaluable insight into your offering's distinctiveness.

Expect Unexpected Market Opportunities

Once you introduce your product, it may attract very different customers than you expected. Examine this carefully as these new and unexpected customers might point to another market opportunity or an even better primary market.

The software company, Broadvision, was founded in 1993 with a mission of enabling interactive cable TV. By the late 1990s, the company was focused almost exclusively on enabling Internet ecommerce sites.

Lego, the well-known children's building block company, discovered a successful niche in the model-building marketplace for older children. While selling toy kits, they found that they were in fact selling permanent models for hobbyists. Lego expanded on this notion and now offers a website that allows users to customize and design their own Lego models. This focus not only expanded their market base, it also created an online community that garnered more enthusiasm for the products.

Are You a Category of One?

You may be looking to "create" a market—to be the first entrant into a particular field. Begin by reviewing your company's non-standard successes. Look at the times your customers have asked you to customize solutions or create entirely new products.

CREATING YOUR VALUE PROPOSITION

These customer requests are by definition unmet market needs. The extent and depth of the opportunity should be examined carefully. How much of a particular unmet need is both repeatable and indicative of a larger market? This may be an opportunity to create a product category of your own as suggested by Joe Calloway in *Becoming a Category of One*. Calloway writes that the answer to combating the crowded marketplace is to create your own product category, ensuring that your company is the only one that can do what you say you do. Easy to conceptualize and much harder to execute. We will look at this more in depth in the *Position to Win* section.

However, there is the risk of mistaking a single specific customer request for a completely new market need. This is often the result of mutual ignorance: both you and your customer are unaware of other vendors who can successfully satisfy the "unmet need." This would become apparent if you were to roll out a new offering or marketing campaign without understanding the (seemingly new) target market opportunity as completely as practical or possible. You can mitigate this risk with due diligence and appropriate market research[11].

In short, the non-standard request **may be** a new and lucrative opportunity. Whatever the case may be, focus on your value proposition. Focus on how it will be relevant to a particular customer in a specific market context. In what group or groups do these customers lie? Identify the best fit with the highest probability of success and put your hypothesis into action.

Is this art or science? Most people who do this work would probably agree that it is both.

Test Your Proposition

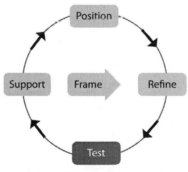

Creating I³ Value Propositions

O nce you have refined your **offering concept statement** and initial **value proposition**, challenge these again against the I³ factors. To what extent will your **target audience** view the product as *Innovative, Indispensable* and *Inspirational*? In addition to testing these against your own experiences and point-of-view, get as much outside validation as possible, given your context (time, talent and other resources.)

Research Within Your Reach

Testing the value proposition is a two-stage undertaking and how much you do at each stage depends on your resources:

- **Prior to launch or final commitments**: For example, online surveys, focus groups, a workshop or extensive personal surveys and other formal market research approaches.

- **"Live ammo" testing**: You're out in the marketplace and you need to understand more than just sales results. Think about how to get honest and candid feedback on your offering from real prospects and customers.

The point here is this: test as much as you can, given your constraints (time, people, budget). Oracle Corp. can and does spend millions of dollars annually on syndicated (published) market research and has a global team focused on understanding short, medium and long-term trends and competitive responses.

CREATING YOUR VALUE PROPOSITION

So, if you're not an Oracle, then leverage your client base, employees who understand the industries you're in, Google, tradeshows, blogs and every bit of news and information that flows around your market space.

The chart on the next page helps organize these resources around key questions that help clarify and validate your offering concept. Ask these questions or compare them to the perspectives of key clients, team and other information resources.

Specifically:

- How well received will our Offering Concept Statement be?

- Which competitors most "sound" like us?

- Which of our features are most attractive to our prospects?

Simple market research guidelines

Typical Verification Questions	Clients	Employees	Industry Venues	Internet Research
How well received will our Offering Concept Statement be?	Actually describe your plans to friendly clients with whom you can engage in candid conversations	Formally ask employees with inside (your target market) industry experience	Review magazines, blogs, etc. that you can peruse to find the Offering Corollary—where they have mentioned the need your offering addresses	Search for Key phrases for the Offering Concept Statement and Offering Corollary
Which Competitors most "sound" like us?	Ask your customers; review recent losses.	Ask employees who worked for competitors in last 6 to 18 months	Review magazines, blogs, etc.	Look up and chart competitors' sites directly
What features are most attractive to our prospects?	Ask your customers	AVOID inside-out examination on this—and don't ask your engineers	Review magazines, blogs, etc.	Look for comparisons performed by respected authorities.

CREATING YOUR VALUE PROPOSITION

Staying Grounded in Your Market's Environment

Always think in terms of validating your value proposition in the overall context of your target market's environment. Examine all the pieces touched on in the go-to-market process: does our value proposition fit with the marketplace as well as competitors' offerings and other available alternatives?

Articulate the I³ Value Proposition as quickly as possible and circulate the message both within and outside your organization to people who are favorably predisposed to your company. Take the refined message to real customers and engage in conversations with senior-level executives about what your product offering will do for them. If resources are available, present the value proposition to respected industry analysts and refine your message further.

As a practical matter, using the following Test Grid with trusted "clear thinkers" inside and outside of your organization could prove to be a simple, inexpensive, direct and valuable exercise. How does your value proposition hold up against this test? What **proof** do you have that target customers believe these claims to be true?

VALUE PROP

I³ Test Grid

1. Describe Your Target Market

Major Industry	Industry Segment	Company Size (revenue/headcount)	Geography

2. Your Offering Concept Statement

3. Describe Your Offering's I³ Factors

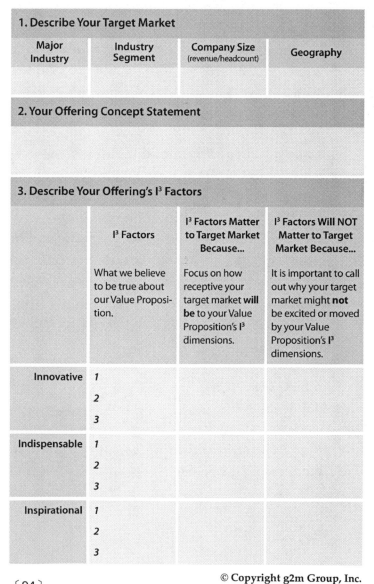

	I³ Factors	I³ Factors Matter to Target Market Because...	I³ Factors Will NOT Matter to Target Market Because...
	What we believe to be true about our Value Proposition.	Focus on how receptive your target market **will be** to your Value Proposition's I³ dimensions.	It is important to call out why your target market might **not** be excited or moved by your Value Proposition's I³ dimensions.
Innovative	1		
	2		
	3		
Indispensable	1		
	2		
	3		
Inspirational	1		
	2		
	3		

How Long Do You Keep on Testing?

When will you know the value proposition is right? How long should you take before the window of opportunity closes? You cannot refine the value proposition beyond your ability to test it in the marketplace. Otherwise, you are just guessing. Admittedly, a seasoned "gut" (say 20 years experience in a given industry) counts a great deal, however, fortunes have been lost when a "veteran" realizes too late that the game has fundamentally changed and cherished rules have been altered.

Having said that, and with appropriate caution, you do have to *get the show on the road*. You could spend an indefinite amount of time refining your proposition and you will lose precious market entry time. So, the answer to the timing question is: verify as much as you can before compromising the opportunity itself by not launching. In other words, stop testing when the risk of **not going** exceeds the risk of not being 100% right.

What's Next?

Ask yourself: *Have we looked at the marketplace to understand our firm's position as well as its competitors? Is our message grounded — built on a solid, factual foundation? Are we ready to commit to our I³ Value Proposition?*

If so, it is possible that you have framed, refined and tested a powerful value proposition—**a message "core"** that feeds your direct sales, field marketing and overall execution plans. You should now have a value proposition that conveys a promise of benefits that are Innovative, Indispensable and Inspirational.

However, will your company be the one to reap the harvest of the market interest and excitement generated by your message? If your product offered "instant teleportation," the market would become excited about the promise of airport-free transportation. Would the market be excited about the prospect of buying this service from **your company**? To ensure that your company benefits from introducing your fresh, useful and exciting value proposition, it needs something more—it needs a Corporate Foundation.

Support Your Proposition

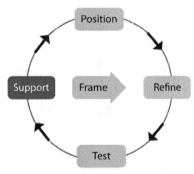

Creating I³ Value Propositions

The Corporate Foundation is the "support" element in the model for I³. It *connects your company* to your value proposition.

VALUE PROP

Let's review where you are in the process:

- You looked at your target market and framed the value proposition with that market in mind.

- You tested the value proposition and concluded that that your target customer will receive the **product or service concept** as Innovative, Indispensable and Inspirational.

- So, why should a customer trust *your company* as the best choice to fulfill the promises conveyed in your value proposition?

The truth is that your messaging strategy might do a great job of educating your target market as to the possibilities implicit in your value proposition without necessarily anchoring those possibilities to your specific company. Think about *"carry **all your music** in one beautifully compact and easy to use device…"* or *"…why not **just log into** your sales force automation software—today—without buying, installing and paying huge sums…"*

The above are just two simple examples of firms that made these offers before Apple and Salesforce.com leveraged them into huge successes for themselves.

CREATING YOUR VALUE PROPOSITION

Why you? Why your product? A well-communicated I[3] Value Proposition can compel your prospect to eagerly seek the value from an incumbent vendor ("can you do this?") or to seek out alternatives (RFPs, for instance). This is why your I[3] Value Proposition requires a Corporate Foundation. The Foundation ensures your firm reaps the harvest—the sale after raising your prospect's consciousness regarding what's possible: the promised benefits that form your value proposition.

Know Who You Are

I worked as a project management consultant to one of the largest legal services organizations in the world leading a significant IT integration project. In the midst of my project, an e-business consultancy asked me to join them as their chief marketing officer. It was a significant transition leveraging my experiences and abilities in new and exciting ways.

I knew my current client was looking at its overall technology and e-business strategy, but at the time, they only knew me as the "IT Guy." In order to continue to do business with them, I had to prove that my new company and I were more than just a technical resource. They asked me in to sit in on one of their e-business meetings, and I knew it was the time to show them that we could deliver what we claimed we could deliver.

During the meeting, I asked the right questions about e-business strategy and made it clear that I could help them. Before I knew it, I (in my new firm) was lead advisor to their new e-business program.

Sometimes, you need to morph your identity to keep up with business. This doesn't mean changing who you are, but changing how others (your target market) perceive you. However, you have to be ready to back it up by *demonstrating* you can do what you say you can do. More importantly, your clients have to be ready and willing to see you in this light.

Xerox tried to sell personal computers and failed miserably. Why? They didn't make a good enough case to the market to look at them as a relevant PC provider. When the market isn't ready for your new capability, you won't succeed. In my case, I had to lead my client to see my credibility and capabilities in a new light. They were used to thinking of me as a "technologist," and I had to train them to look at me as a "strategist."

The Corporate Foundation

You must create your firm's Corporate Foundation to ensure that customers view you as the most credible vendor for your offering. The Corporate Foundation includes three time-related dimensions or factors:

CREATING YOUR VALUE PROPOSITION

Credibility: There has to be a reason to believe that your company can deliver the promised value in your value proposition. Credibility points toward your **past** successes, using them as a foundation for why customers can rely on your firm in the future. Credibility sounds like, "Over the past ten years we have served the leading financial services firms in …"

Cost-effectiveness: This dimension represents the hard-core **present**. This means pricing the product sharply, relative to its market and solution category. This is a moving target, as competitors vie for your customers' attention with creative bundles, disruptive technologies or outright attempts to "buy the business" with unsustainable loss-leader pricing. Cost-effectiveness will usually be manifested as a comparative statement justifying the investment against either another expense area or a competitor, "Our product will reduce your energy expenses by 20%, paying for itself in 24 months." Or, "Compared to XYZ Company, our network hubs reduce operational support by half, paying for themselves in 12 months…"

VALUE PROP

Capability: While credibility looks to the past, capability points toward the **future**. Capability says, "We're ready to serve you now and we have the **capacity** to make and fulfill that promise." Capability often sounds like facts and figures: "We have 20 offices with 100 technicians on call, 24x7."

The part of the Corporate Foundation that usually gets the most attention is cost-effectiveness. Cost-effectiveness is relative to the customer and their expectations of the product's value. Boeing's Dreamliner represents a multi-billion dollar investment for airlines that buy it—and it is a breakthrough in cost-effectiveness. The product's price must align with what customers view as affordable for your particular value proposition.

You can communicate cost-effectiveness as simply price/performance, but developing an ROI (Return on Investment) and/or TCO (Total Cost of Ownership) "story" is the wiser course of action for big-ticket products or services. In high-tech, this is a mature practice, but with varying degrees of success due to eroding customer confidence in the accuracy or consistency of vendors' claims. Nonetheless, every offering should have some value/cost "touch-points" articulated as part of the Corporate Foundation of its value proposition.

A Simple Corporate Foundation Checklist

1. Describe Your Target Market

Major Industry	Industry Segment	Company Size (revenue/headcount)	Geography

2. Your Offering Concept Statement

3. Describe Your Offering's I³ Factors

Innovative	Indispensable	Inspirational
1	1	1
2	2	2
3	3	3

4. Corporate Foundation

What in your company's past supports its unique ability to deliver the above I³ factors?	What in your company's pricing and other supporting evidence points to its unique ability to deliver the above I³ factors cost-effectively?	What about your company's resources (people, technology, partners, etc.) support its unique ability to deliver the above I³ factors?

Almost There...

I developed I³ as the heart of a holistic approach to go-to-market messaging. Built on an understanding of your marketplace, the I³ Value Proposition creates a targeted and specific value offering that is supported by its Corporate Foundation—your company's ability to deliver on the promises in its value offering.

"Differentiate your company and your product." Easy to say, hard to define and extremely challenging to do well. I³ provides a framework and test criteria to work out your offering's differentiation in terms that matter to your prospects. In short, elevate your firm and your product into the elite of your industry by asking the right questions of the right target market. This means conveying a results-based message to prospects. Approach markets with the right value proposition, connecting and creating a spark. Ground and empower that value proposition with a credible, capable and cost-effective corporate story.

Use the I³ Value Proposition as the key to open the door to your target market.

But...

What about competitors?

Position to Win

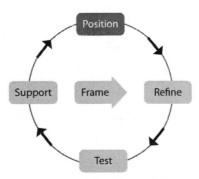

Creating I³ Value Propositions

Positioning is a concept that marketing strategists, consultants and academics continue to define and redefine. For our purposes, I'll prefer to cast positioning as a principle that operates and is experienced from your **target market's point of view**.

It is a reflection of how potential customers view and evaluate specific offerings in comparison to that offering's competitors. Positioning is based on attributes that are important in the mind of buyers. Marketers must understand this mental landscape (from their target market's point of view) and align their offering accordingly.

Positioning analysis and mapping takes into account not only your product offering and its competitors, but perhaps most importantly, those **attributes that most matter** to a specific group of customers.

The classic positioning grid, often seen in the high-tech industry as "magic quadrants[12]," is a well-known and well-used tool of marketers in every industry. Typically, we score products from high to low on two or more product attributes, placing them into value quadrants, with the upper right representing a "best" position and the lower left, "worst" or "weakest." (See Sample Positioning Grid on the next page.)

In the mind of prospects, your company will be positioned one way or another—whether you are strategic or purposeful about it or not. The key is that you *can* be strategic and make decisions to *influence* the position of the product through product development and marketing communications efforts.

CREATING YOUR VALUE PROPOSITION

Sample Positioning Grid

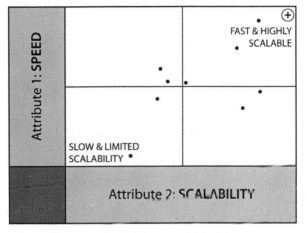

⊕ = Fastest and Most Scalable Solution

Companies fall into a trap of mapping themselves in a theoretical "hot-zone," based on two particular attributes that may reflect well on the product offering, but then fail to verify them as having significant or **highest meaning** to their target customers. In other words, an "inside-out" view can usually find two attributes that your team can get excited about and even believe it can establish leadership in—even if the attributes are not real priorities for your current or target customer.

However, if your product's attributes are not a high priority for your intended market, but in fact represent a true distinctive, they may point to another market where they would be more highly prized. As a result, your market research must identify the most important attributes on which to base your offering's messaging platform.

Keeping Your Position Real

Organizations often convince themselves that they have a position in the marketplace based solely on the intellectual or "inside-out" exercise mentioned above, when the actual position held is quite different. It's the trap of "idealizing" your position. The business landscape is littered with countless failed products launched on the strength of their originators' confidence in their own assumptions. For every Al Neuharth (who launched USA Today in the face of a chorus of skeptics) who gets to "laugh last," there are many more who end up blindsided by a fast-moving and increasingly demanding market.

Before the Apple iPod's remarkable success, there were several MP3 players on the market, including fine efforts by iRiver and Diamond Multimedia. By choosing to view each other's MP3 players as their primary competition, these companies neglected to acknowledge that in reality their true competition was the **alternative** to an MP3 player, namely, the status quo—consumers using CDs and playing them on traditional portable CD players.

CREATING YOUR VALUE PROPOSITION

At the time, **potential** MP3 player customers still preferred to keep their music collections on compact discs. Music listeners did not have a reason to believe that MP3 players were sufficiently superior to the compact disc players, in complete solution terms. Many prospects found the process of ripping CDs, uncertain licensing (i.e., Napster) and other hassle factors contributed to a "wait and see" stance. In contrast, Apple's iPod created a simple way for anyone to digitize and carry his or her entire music library. The company moved quickly and fired all bullets with a stellar marketing campaign and a sharply positioned I³ Value Proposition.

How do you keep it real? How do you stretch and cast a vision—by definition, ahead of the market and yet grounded in reality? In large part, it is by careful testing and, more importantly, by being willing to hear bad news early. As mentioned before, bad news could simply mean that you're targeting the wrong market or niche. Of course, it could mean, "Stop! Pigs aren't going to fly and neither is your product!"

Sometimes, market reality just doesn't seem to make sense. For instance, Tablet PCs. Why wouldn't everyone want to be able to write out their thoughts on their laptop in the same way as they do their paper notepad? Yet, the market repeatedly has voted this category of technology a non-starter at worst, or a highly specialized (and small) niche.

In the mind of every potential customer looking to solve a problem, there is a short list of possible alternatives (vendors, solution categories or "work-arounds"). Positioning means that you want to be on that short list, in the specific situation your solution addresses. Positioning seeks answers to the question—"*How do I appear on the top of that list?*"

Where Are You on the Positioning Ladder?

The business classic, Positioning: *The Battle for Your Mind*, by Al Ries and Jack Trout, succinctly captured the practical aspects of positioning for any product or service and how to test for it. Their book popularized the reality of category "ladders." For example, they cited the concept of "rungs" on the ladder occupied by two or three leading brands of toothpaste. At the time of their writing, they noted Colgate, Crest and few others. Marketers today generally accept that prospects allocate a very limited number of "rungs" per category ladder in order to organize their worldview and make easier and less stressful purchasing decisions.

The key point is that **categories** are how buyers structure their thinking around many options within any given grouping of products and services. I have found that the same dynamic holds for commercial products and services. Although computer servers and ERP software are not impulse buys—positioning theory and practice holds that large organizations still have limited time to evaluate a seemingly unlimited number of competitors.

To put it in more contemporary and business-focused terms, let's use some recent examples: Think about *Internet browsers*—what comes to mind? Internet Explorer, Firefox, maybe Safari. *Word Processing?* Microsoft Word and... *Toothpaste?* Colgate, Crest and...

Positioning is not simply an intellectual exercise. It reflects a key decision-making dynamic in the minds of your buyer—especially business buyers. In fact, business-to-business brand and product positioning can be as much a nuanced art as consumer branding.

The key question then is: *How do you get on the short list?* More specifically, *How do you get on the **right** short list?*

Part of the answer is: *if you want to own a particular product category—and it has an established leader, create a completely new one.* We can define this new category by a key service or product attribute. For example, Dell broke the IBM dominance over Intel-based PCs with a

Direct-to-Buyer model. This made them the leader in directly procured PCs. Corporate America said "Yes" in a big way and Dell was on its way to redefining what selling PCs was about.

This worked for Dell because you must be in (or create) a category that answers genuine customer needs. Using one of Ries and Trout's examples, consumers had the option of buying simple toothpaste and a few distinct flavors within that category. Today, however, new brands have created an entirely new category of teeth whiteners with much higher price points. Line extensions or extending a brand over other, loosely related products (a practice that Ries and Trout often reference as a great blight on modern marketing) only add to the confusion and challenge for buyers.

Combining "service dimensions" is how the airlines, Southwest and Jet Blue, do it. Both position themselves as **hassle-free** and **low-cost airlines**. They occupy a new category of friendly service **and** price leadership. As of this writing, whether this is a sustainable business model is a point of considerable conjecture on Wall Street. Jet Blue customers (including me) hope they manage to keep the formula intact.

CREATING YOUR VALUE PROPOSITION

In some cases, you may want to align your product within an established category to make it easier to highlight what you provide or how your product fits into a company's budget for that category (an example would be training services). For business products and services, it all circles back to I³. How is your offer new, truly useful and exciting—for a specific market?

Where does your I³ Value Proposition position you in the marketplace? Will you end up on the short lists of your target audience?

Hypothesis, framing, refining, testing and positioning—all based on as keen a grasp of your target market's needs as possible—should yield a sharp and viable value proposition. Communicating that value proposition and making it easily understood is a major consideration and is the subject of our next section.

Simplify for Understanding

At the end of each pass through your value prop, you must simplify. A few practical steps will help you get to the *pearl of great price* of your offering. By this, I mean highlighting and not hiding the true main point (the net-net "goodness") that proves most compelling to prospects.

Simplify by reducing the number of features or benefits in your story. Don't reduce the actual features that make up your offering, but reduce the number of features you communicate. This may seem counter-intuitive, in that it is easy to feel that "more is more."

However, given the crowded marketplace and ever increasing levels of market noise, it is a strategic imperative to deliver a simply understood story to your market.

I have found that the more complex the product, the less effective it is to deliver the proverbial "fire hose" of information to an already overwhelmed audience. The point of reducing the number of features communicated is twofold: to force you to evaluate which features really matter to prospects and to enable you to deliver those points more clearly.

Simplify by reducing the number of words you use to communicate a feature. You can use simpler language such as "this means..." and "this doesn't mean..." to frame key points. There is a time and place to introduce the twenty-page PDF with detailed schematics and power charts. It's just not at the front end of the communication and sales process.

Simplify by reducing the use of jargon and dense wording. I don't mean language that's simplistic or condescending—I **do** mean language understood by a nontechnical executive who understands business terms and concepts.

CREATING YOUR VALUE PROPOSITION

Finally, simplify by reducing the number and depth of slides in your PowerPoint presentation. The old adage of "tell them what you're going to tell them; tell them; then tell them what you told them" is a simple and still effective way to approach any presentation. The middle part is where many business product and services companies fall into their own snare of complexity.

PowerPoint is a wonderful tool to capture new ideas—and is also a collector of "dust balls" of too many ideas and details. We've all sat through (or given) one-hour PowerPoint talks that left everyone, including the speaker, more confused than when the talk began.

You can clarify and simplify any presentation (or document) by taking this simplification test:

- Can I capture my essential offering in one slide? You can state your Value Proposition (using the Offering Concept Statement) and add a few short clarifying bullets—but that's it!

- Can I describe what my product does in one slide of less than 50 words (adding up all the bullets)?

- Can I describe on one slide what our product/service brings to the market that is new, useful and exciting (your offering's I^3 dimensions)?

VALUE PROP

- Can I describe on one slide what in our company's history points to our distinct ability to deliver this specific value proposition (Credibility from your Corporate Foundation)?

- Can I describe on one slide a way of looking at our offering financially that is compelling—emphasizing a key financial benefit or dynamic unique to your offering (Cost Effectiveness from your Corporate Foundation)?

- Can I describe on one slide what in our present people, processes and resources points to our distinct ability to deliver this specific value proposition (Capability from your Corporate Foundation)?

Be direct. Be clear. In short—keep it short. Your prospects will appreciate it and understand your story better as a result.

If your primary channel is direct sales (either your own team or a partner's), then the next section will help you bridge these concepts into on-the-ground tools that will make a positive difference in your market success.

Building the Bridge

*Drive "big ticket" sales by
connecting value propositions
to sales conversations.*

Building the Bridge

In this section, I will describe and apply the concept of Sales Cases to your I³ Value Proposition.

We will discuss why even a great value proposition is not enough and why you must extend your message planning and development to your direct sales efforts as well. We will look at the five Sales Cases that every direct sales organization should be prepared to make and briefly review how the Sales Cases fit into Sales Methodologies and how to use Sales Cases to create conversations that close deals.

A Great Value Proposition
is Not Enough

P erhaps you have framed, refined, tested, supported and positioned your I³ Value Proposition. Your marketing program does a great and thorough job articulating the "goodness" of your offering via your materials, events and advertising. Your sales team is talented, trained and managed professionally.

You are confident that your program is persuasive and effective in motivating your **target audience** to select, or at least, nurture an interest in your offering. For example, if your product represents a radically less expensive way to accomplish a critical task, your program emphasizes that fact and connects with prospects who appreciate that feature.

So far, so good—this is fundamental sales and marketing—energized by an I³ Value Proposition. But, what good is a killer value prop if your targeted **decision makers** don't hear it, understand it or see why it should matter to them? If your value proposition is great on the proverbial drawing board—even great in your brochures and web site—but is not conveyed or contextualized for the **real buyers** you need to connect with, your program will fall short of expectations or fail outright.

In most cases, the application of your promise of benefits (the essence of your value proposition) to **specific client situations** is a task that falls to your direct sales force. As Francisco Dao, founder of California-based executive coaching and consulting firm Strategy and Performance, noted, "No strategy can be fully developed if the primary customer-facing employees—the salespeople—don't adjust their skills and tactics to fully exploit that strategy."

This is more than just an issue of having great marketing materials, however powerful you may believe yours to be. You have to go beyond "marcom" and translate the innovative, indispensable and inspirational attributes of your offering into the language of decision makers. This will most typically be around business, financial, technical and other concerns of key stakeholders considering your offer. Developing and training on "most likely" discussions with decision makers would connect the work done developing a value proposition with the work done developing and equipping your sales team.

Messaging (and by this I mean a complete messaging strategy, from branding to sales conversations) can and should be developed carefully and **proactively** and inclusive of the direct sales experience. Why leave any part of it vulnerable to the variations and inconsistencies of a sales team—regardless of how well trained they may be?

Complex Products Do Not Sell Themselves

Even products with the most expertly crafted value proposition, *even one framed as an I^3 Value Proposition*, still require a human element to connect the dots for prospects.

The direct sales function (and for our purposes, this includes business development and alliance partners who negotiate or create deals) has to connect the value of your product and the needs and requirements of your prospects, in the context of each prospect's decision-making criteria and processes. Pip Coburn, author of *The Change Function*, further argues that customers don't just need a good reason, but a great reason to change their current behaviors. People naturally want to resist change. It is crisis, an intense need for something different and better, which breeds change.

It is critical that customers perceive the difference in the solution you are offering and **see how they would value and prefer it to their current way of getting the job done** as well as prefer it to similar offerings.

This means the sales challenge is not limited to just beating competitors. If your offering represents a fresh and new thought, it likely requires some changes in current practices as well. This places your offering right up against the comfort of the **status-quo**, which is the often-overlooked **real** competitor that a vendor must address to succeed. Making these distinctions and navigating this process is what top sales performers do well.

However, even the sales core competency of developing relationships, can present distinct challenges as well. In their book, *Creating Relational Capital*, John Holland and Ed Wallace note, "Some salespeople instinctively possess natural people and relationship skills that help them navigate through these 21st Century dynamics, while others thrash about and are never able to 'get it.'"

Being great with people, while a skill that can and should be developed, is certainly not a given—and is not enough to close complex deals in any scalable or predictable way. Yet, many organizations rely on "powers of persuasion." This may certainly work in a given situation but it is not an effective go-to-market philosophy. *"I know it is not what they need or want—but we'll just change their minds."*

Perhaps you should pack your offering with as many desirable features as possible. While a strategy many late entrants attempt, *feature parity* alone does not differentiate, no matter how crammed your product is with the latest bells and whistles—if they're the same bells and whistles as your competitors offer.

There are no shortcuts: you have to find out **what your customers really want or need** and focus on delivering something of value against that need. Your marketing message, positioning, branding and differentiation are crucial keys to the sale, yet these messages hold stronger value when translated into practical language that your direct sales force can bring into sales calls as part of their overall tool kit. To put it another way, you must answer the simple question: *"How do we sell this message when we're face to face?"*

Start with a key idea, expressed as differentiated attributes (new, useful and exciting), supported by a corporate "story" (credible, capable and cost-effective) that validates the idea and connect the dots to your customer's decision criteria (business, financial, technical, process and competitive) and you will have a winning formula.

Not a magic formula—but a foundation with which you can enter and win new markets.

Building the Bridge
with Sales Cases

E very day, you or your sales team map critical connections between your offering concept (why you and your organization believe your offering is unique and valuable to a target market) and specific sales situations. Prepare your sales teams to **make** those connections using the Sales Cases as a model (the Cases were mentioned at the beginning of this book and are an extension of your messaging platform from strategy and product concept to direct sales support).

Think of Sales Cases as logical "buckets" for conversations your sales personnel will likely engage in before being able to close any one deal. Where developing an I^3 Value Proposition helps frame, focus and tighten your strategy and message, Sales Cases **anticipate** the areas of concern that prospects (based on your organizational and industry experience) will require you to address.

Another way to look at Sales Cases is to think of a legal proceeding—one in which you have to prove something beyond a reasonable doubt. Ask the question, *"What case will I have to make to **prove the merit** of my offering for **this** customer?"* Notice, it is proving the merit "for" this customer and not "to" this customer. The goal is not merely convincing your prospect of your case, but actually finding and substantiating the actual merit of your offering in each of the five case-dimensions. To illustrate, note the message progression chart below.

	Product Messaging		Company Messaging	Direct Sales
Your Product's Story	Offering Concept Statement	I^3 Attributes		
Your Company's Story			Corporate Foundation	
Your Prospect's Concerns				Sales Cases

Think about the sales calls you and your team have engaged in. At the beginning of a specific campaign, you probably try to establish your company as a "player" within your target market as evidenced by years in that industry, specific expertise or client references. Further, in a complex sale, you will ascertain your prospect's strategic direction and call out how your firm's direction is consistent with theirs. A seasoned sales rep will think about how to articulate her solution as making great business sense for her prospect. This natural flow is the essence of the Business Case, the first of five Sales Cases, which are:

- The Business Case

- The Financial Case

- The Technical Case

- The Competitive Case

- The Decision Process Case

The Sales Cases Described

The following are high-level profiles for each Case. Think about how you could apply these concepts to the real-world situations you encounter in your target markets.

VALUE PROP

- *The Business Case* considers your prospect's mission and the issues and processes they are trying to resolve, enhance, or enable. The business case establishes the **overall business logic** behind choosing your solution or product. This case centers on concepts such as mission, vision and what comprises the client's biggest "win." These conversations may seem mostly "C" suite in nature, but are actually themes that should be addressed at all levels.

- *The Technical Case* takes into account your prospect's ability to **absorb** your offering. It is customer centered and focuses on how they will evaluate your offering's **capabilities**, in several technical dimensions. This is where you would explore issues such as personnel, legacy systems (in IT), facilities and ease of integration.

- *The Financial Case* analyzes a prospect's financial targets, thresholds and expectations for purchases. This is more than a budget conversation, but a dialogue that gets to the heart of why it is **good business** to select your offering. This should be developed as an ROI or Total Cost of Ownership (TCO) story that is relatively easy to present. While senior executives and the CFO may be the primary point of contact on this dimension, any budget-focused manager will likely want to engage in discussions regarding the financial impact of your offering.

- *The Competitive Case* examines the strengths and weaknesses of your organization and specific offering against your competitors in language that is non-confrontational. It reveals an understanding of the **landscape of options** your customer is considering. Your prospects **know** you are not the only game in town. Preparing for this case gives you an opportunity to frame the discussion your prospect is **already** having internally.

- *The Decision Case* defines how a selling organization works with clients to enable them to make informed decisions regarding the solution or product they are considering. Simply, how you work with prospects to enhance the selection and **buying experience**. The Decision Case looks at your prospect's highest value requirement, assurance of fulfillment, and considers how your offering either reduces or increases different risk dimensions. All sized organizations have become increasingly formal in this evaluation and marketing and sales organizations should be conversant in Risk Management language as a result.

The I^3 **Value Proposition** calls out the specific promises your product makes and the attributes that set that product apart, and the **Corporate Foundation** establishes why your company is best suited to offer that product. The **Sales Cases** anticipates the five customer-oriented decision criteria that are used in most complex sales situations.

Integrating Sales Cases

Think about your offering in the language of these five Cases and develop training, presentations, a cheat sheet or other tools to give your salespeople practical guidance in how to use them. Use formats and language they are likely to understand and find motivating. The Sales Cases should **supplement** your marketing materials and literature, providing a specific resource to aid sales people in **creating conversations that close deals**, a concept we will explore shortly.

VALUE PROP

The following model illustrates the flow **from** an I³ Value Proposition used for developing strategy and marketing messaging **to** the Sales Cases used to empower sales conversations.

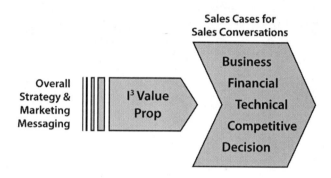

Of course, Sales Cases are **not** a sales methodology, *per se*. Excellent sales processes such as Customer Centric Selling, Miller Heiman, SPIN Selling, Value Selling and many others are available and have proven valuable to all size organizations. A walk down the aisle at Barnes & Nobles or Borders Bookstores will offer the motivated manager a plethora of sales advice. Larger organizations commit significant resources to hiring process-oriented sales managers and training their large direct sales forces in the finer art of complex selling and account management. A **sales methodology** plugs sales professionals into a process and provides consistent "pipeline" visibility to sales management. Additionally, these systems enhance salespeople's productivity and their overall success rate in tangible, measurable ways. These systems enhance the skill and approach of your professionals, as will their experience. The question, however, is how to ensure **all** your sales professionals engage meeting after meeting and proposal after proposal, with a better and **consistently effective** message.

In contrast, Sales Cases are a **set of messaging tools** that experienced sales executives can use in their day-to-day sales efforts, within the parameters of their organizations' existing sales methodology. They will help you **shorten sales cycles and close more business**. The "big idea" is that these tools are **complementary** to a formal sales process and not a replacement for it. The Sales Cases should be included as part of your internal collateral or be used as a new way to communicate product collateral. They can be a set of discussions and training times with your direct sales staff, as well.

"Doesn't sales and marketing collateral accomplish this?" Sales collateral (web site, events and other marketing tools) are surely part of the picture, but Sales Cases equip sales professionals to engage in specific conversations in order for decision makers (whether technical buyers or final, financial buyers) to say Yes!

VALUE PROP

Sales Cases should be **designed centrally** by a management of marketing function and **applied situationally** by your sales professionals. Marketing and Sales management both need to acknowledge the strategic "big picture" vision **and** the value of converting the conceptual (positioning, differentiation, other value elements) parts of your company's go-to-market program specifically for sales professionals as **tools they can use**.

The alternative to proactively developing Sales Cases is to depend on individual sales professionals to handle and **translate** your "big picture" messaging strategy on their own. Anyone who has managed a sales team understands that not all salespeople are able to deliver complex messaging on the strength of their personal skills alone. I have worked with talented and competent sales professionals, but few, if any, had the time or management support for accomplishing this task on their own.

The bottom line: **someone** should create and review Sales Cases for your company's offerings.

BUILDING THE BRIDGE

Sales Cases Recap

The Business Case considers your prospect's mission and the issues and processes they are trying to resolve, enhance, or enable.

The Financial Case analyzes a prospect's financial targets, thresholds and expectations for purchases.

The Technical Case takes into account your prospect's ability to absorb your offering.

The Competitive Case examines your strengths and weaknesses against your competitors in language that is non-confrontational.

The Decision Case defines how the selling organization works with clients to enable them to make informed decisions.

Creating Conversations
that Close Deals

What does a Sales Case look like?

Are they sales scripts?

Are they a new type of marketing collateral?

Are Sales Cases a new form of training?

The answer to the above questions is Yes, and…

If we can capture the essential *net-new*, *net-useful* and *net-wow*! attributes of an offering… if we can support that story with an understanding of how our company's past (credibility), present and future (capability) and pricing (cost-effectiveness) position us uniquely to make the offering…then, why wouldn't we pursue **opportunities to discuss** the business, financial and technical reasons we can address the real-world needs of our (carefully chosen) target market?

These are conversations you can prepare your reps to handle—and handle consistently—using Sales Cases as an outline. By sales conversations, I mean the many meetings and interactions your sales professionals conduct with the many stakeholders typically involved in purchasing larger capital goods and services, ranging from software to computers to jet engines—and the service contracts that go with them.

Ideally, the Cases illustrate how to articulate your products' marketing message in actual sales discussions. Sales Cases anticipate the nature and flow of specific types of conversations (business, financial, technical, competitive and decision process) that arise throughout your typical sales cycles. Quite simply, documenting, training and monitoring the use of Sales Cases can help an organization drive greater consistency from their entire team.

Doug Crisman, a friend, mentor and long-time IT industry sales and marketing executive, often observed that most sales teams could be divided into three groups. First, a small percentage can map strategic marketing messages into specific sales points. These become top performers and consistently adapt to changing market conditions, product introductions and organizational shifts. The second and largest group require (and hopefully accept and appreciate) varying degrees of help from their sales managers in making these connections. Of course, the third group would be a (hopefully) smaller number who never "get it."

The reality is that most sales team's abilities will likely fall along the bell curve noted by Crisman and not every salesperson can skillfully bridge the gap between marketing materials and the sales call. That is why Sales Cases **make these connections explicit**, offering a map for the salesperson, leading to the destination: closing the deal. This map should document customer concerns and how your products address them.

The Sales Case document would highlight your new (innovative), useful (indispensable) and exciting (inspirational) attributes across business, financial, technical, decision and competitive dimensions. (See Sales Cases/Worksheet/Matrix at the end of this chapter.) Develop an "alignment statement" for each case—a general sentence or two that conveys how your offering aligns with the concern that Case addresses. For example, for the Business Case of a product used by environmentally conscious companies, an alignment statement would look like: "Our product, CleanFare, is a result of our commitment to green production methods."

You will find many uses for your Sales Cases as sales cycles involve many meetings with people at all levels within a prospect organization. Use this format to start thinking about how you can bring your company or product's distinctive elements into specific and likely sales conversations. The power of this is simple—for example, when discussing why your firm aligns with a prospect from a Business Mission or Vision point of view, your sales professional can remind them of new or strikingly innovative features your product contains that reflects that mission.

In short, Sales Cases take your marketing message down to ground level, ensuring that high-level and strategic marketing ideas survive the descent into the sales trenches. They make certain that your corporate and strategic vision, brand and positioning messaging are present in the day-to-day conversations that drive your sales campaigns.

BUILDING THE BRIDGE

Sales Cases Worksheet/Matrix

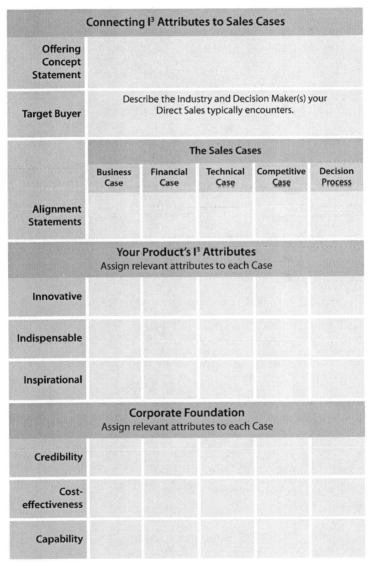

Connecting I³ Attributes to Sales Cases					
Offering Concept Statement					
Target Buyer	Describe the Industry and Decision Maker(s) your Direct Sales typically encounters.				
	The Sales Cases				
	Business Case	Financial Case	Technical Case	Competitive Case	Decision Process
Alignment Statements					
Your Product's I³ Attributes Assign relevant attributes to each Case					
Innovative					
Indispensable					
Inspirational					
Corporate Foundation Assign relevant attributes to each Case					
Credibility					
Cost-effectiveness					
Capability					

The I³ Challenge

Real and Dynamic Differentiation

Some Final Thoughts

A t the beginning of this book, I observed that our world is being "messaged" to death. We are overwhelmed with ads and marketing programs attempting to sell us everything from toilet paper to airplanes. Advertisements are everywhere! Sales pitches are increasingly saturating buyers. Marketing messages are constantly flowing into inboxes, phones, TV—even going to the movies requires exposure to 30 minutes of pre-show infomercials, commercials and endless previews.

VALUE PROP

This phenomenon of message clutter is not without an impact on commercial sales. After all, your buyers are people too. That is, they are juggling messaging in-flow for their personal and professional lives and it has become overwhelming. So much so, that business people, including your buyers, have become increasingly adept at filtering it out.

Given this crowded message-space, **message efficiency** must be a core consideration of your go-to-market plans. I have been making the case that you can explain your company's differentiation most effectively by developing and communicating your message in I^3 terms as described in this book. An I^3 Value Proposition is at the heart of an effective go-to-market framework and critical to the development of a powerful message strategy.

How do you ensure that it will intersect with the needs of your target market and real prospects? Integrate these I^3 concepts into your entire go-to-market strategy—all the way down to a product design that includes inspirational and differentiated features.

A clear validation for your I^3 Value Proposition is that your product sells. While this is an important and seemingly obvious data-point, it may not be enough. Selling and **selling as well as possible** are two different outcomes. Are you leaving money on the table by not leveraging or delivering your message to the highest degree possible?

The following 9 Point Go-To-Market Checklist can help you check your go-to-market and message development efforts:

1. Shape your message to ensure its **staying power**. It must survive the many hands that will tweak, repurpose, reuse and receive it.

2. An I³ Value Proposition is about more than just *being* different, of course—as I³ is also concerned with the **effective delivery** of the *differentiated message* (being *seen* as different.)

3. All differentiation is a state in **a moment in time** and is, by definition, transient and temporary. You can be differentiated today and not even relevant tomorrow—think Polaroid.

4. If you don't see true differentiation in your product when forming your I³ Value Proposition, do something about it before it is too late. Rethink your packaging—reconsider your target market. While you can add differentiation later—it will be more expensive and painful.

5. It is not just your product's attributes that communicate value; your **Corporate Foundation** has to support it. Skipping this step could allow a larger, possibly more credible competitor to "adopt" your I^3 concept and run with it.

6. Avoid the trap of developing positioning in a vacuum or just within the friendly confines of your own team. You have to **understand where you actually are** in the market—and for that, you will need some outside perspectives (your outside board, customers, market analysts, formal market research and trusted advisors.)

7. Stay up to date with the more easily available public information about your industry, competitors and key customers.

8. The average commercial sales professional spends several hundred hours per year talking to prospects and customers—consider the sheer quantity of data and insights not captured. You would do well to **include your sales colleagues** in at least **some** powerful conversations around marketplace realities "on the ground"—not to define strategy, but to *inform* it.

9. **Talk to your customers** often and systematically. By this I don't mean surveys, but candid conversations with them. Ask them what they think about your existing and potential product offerings.

Being different, in meaningful ways—and communicating that difference effectively—must be the cornerstone of your go-to-market strategy. Differentiation that truly matters provides the energy that advances and animates your value proposition—allowing you to turn marketing messages and sales conversations into sales successes.

Please feel free to share your experiences applying the principles in this book with me at Jpalomlno@valueprop.com.

References

Your Message Matters

Christine Canabou, "Advertising, Under Review," *Fast Company*, Issue 57, March 2002.

"12 Timely Recommendations Can Lead to Better Go-to-Market Strategies for IT Providers," Gartner, Inc. 2005.

Alex Wipperfurth, *Brand Hijack* (New York: Portfolio, 2005).

What is I³

Patricia B. Seybold, *Outside Innovation* (Collins, 2006).

The Differentiation Dilemma

Geoff Colvin, "Selling P&G," *Fortune*, http://www.money.cnn.com/magazines/fortune/fortune_archive/2007/09/17/100258870/, September 17, 2007.

Michael Treacy & Fred Wiersema, *The Discipline of Market Leaders* (Perseus Books Group: Expanded edition, January 1997).

Frame Your Proposition

"100 Million iPods Sold," Apple Corporation, http://www.apple.com/pr/library/2007/04/09ipod. html, April 9, 2007.

Chris Pentilla, "Age of the iPod," *Entreprenuer*, January 2006, p. 17-18.

Jena McGregor, "The World's Most Innovative Companies," *BusinessWeek*, May 4, 2007.

Reena Jana, "How To Live Up to the Innovation Hype," NEWSFACTOR.com, http://www.newsfactor.com/story.xhtml?story_id=0110001A6HI8, April 10, 2007.

Julia Chang, "The Power of Design in Building Your Business," *Sales & Marketing* Web Extra. http://www.managesmarter.com/msg/content_display/marketing/e3i47ee107d892405fec19ff8ea98858b0 d, April 27, 2007.

Refine Your Offering Concept

Joe Calloway, *Becoming a Category of One* (Hoboken, NJ: John Wiley & Sons Inc, 2003).

A Great Value Proposition is Not Enough

Francisco Dao, "Why Can't Salespeople Be More Creative?," Inc.com,
http://www.inc.com/resources/sales/articles/20050901/dao.html, June 3, 2007.

Pip Coburn, *The Change Function* (Penguin Group Inc., 2006).

Notes

[1] The Zune did achieve 9% market share in its first year, according to research house NPD. (pg. 32)

[2] As of this writing, Microsoft has released a second generation Zune, with many previous limitations addressed. Almost unique to Microsoft, the company has the depth of capital and marketing perseverance to enter and re-enter markets over years to attain its eventual goal of a number one rank (see Windows NT, Xbox and Office). (pg. 32)

[3] When thinking of Dell on the national stage as a provider of lowest cost laptops and desktops. Local companies might produce less expensive products—but without Dell's service and reputation. (pg. 38)

[4] They understood that a Big Mac ordered in a dirty restaurant, with surly service, would fail. Their point is that maturing markets raise the "acceptable" level for all three dimensions, and these levels are effectively "table stakes" to enter a given market. Differentiation would come from placing an emphasis on one of the three—true Market Leadership. (pg. 39)

[5] The study of the processes involved in the long-distance transmission of computer data—Encarta Dictionary. (pg. 48)

[6] SOA is a design linking business and computational resources on demand in order to deliver desired results for end users or other services. (pg. 70)

[7] Software as a service (SaaS) is a software application delivery model where vendors develop a web-delivered software application and hosts and operates the software for its customers over the Internet. (pg. 70)

[8] As of this writing, Boeing had been experiencing some difficulties with its supply chain—but was confident, along with industry analysts, that the long-term success of the Dreamliner was not in jeopardy. (pg. 72)

[9] In 2004, online auctioneer eBay purchased a 28.4% stake in Craigslist from a former employee—WSJ April 26, 2008. (pg. 73)

[10] Corollary. (n.d.). The American Heritage® Science Dictionary. "A statement that follows with little or no proof required from an already proven statement." From website: http://dictionary.reference.com/browse/corollary. (pg. 80)

[11] Today's web services allow for testing of messages, advertising concepts, surveys and "heads down" research at unprecedented speed and with relatively modest investments. (pg. 87)

[12] Gartner.com: Magic Quadrants and MarketScopes offer visual snapshots of a market's direction, maturity and participants. (pg. 106)

About the Author

Jose Palomino is founder and President of g2m Group, Inc., helping businesses take their ideas, products and services to market faster and more effectively. With over twenty years' leadership experience in the technology and service sectors, Mr. Palomino is a proven strategist, dealmaker and presenter. He has held management, technology, sales and marketing positions at Market Systems International, the Yankee Group, Tandem Computers and the Clearpoint Group—working with industry leaders including IBM, Accenture, Unisys, SAP, General Motors, Chase and Citicorp. Mr. Palomino holds an MBA from Villanova University.

Value Prop is Mr. Palomino's first book.

You can learn more about his work at
www.valueprop.com.

ValueProp.com

Join the **ValueProp.com** community to interact with peers, access tools and extend and deepen your understanding and application of I³ and **Sales Cases**.

Membership is Free for book owners and includes great member features, including:

- Special **"Gift-Forward"** feature—you can personally give a copy of *Value Prop* to a colleague—at no cost to you!

- Special **team pricing** for multiple copies of *Value Prop*

- Downloadable PDF worksheets

- Special Webinars and other training events

- Online assessment tools and other interactive tools that enhance the experience of *Value Prop*

- Take the I³ **Challenge** and find out what your peers think about your *"Killer* Value Prop." Prizes awarded to the top-rated I³ **Challenger**!